Public Goods and Externalities

AGRI-ENVIRONMENTAL POLICY MEASURES IN SELECTED OECD COUNTRIES

Please cite this publication as:
OECD (2015), *Public Goods and Externalities: Agri-environmental Policy Measures in Selected OECD Countries*, OECD Publishing, Paris.
http://dx.doi.org/10.1787/9789264239821-en

ISBN 978-92-64-23979-1 (print)
ISBN 978-92-64-23982-1 (PDF)

Photo credits: Cover © Pgiam/istockphoto.com

Corrigenda to OECD publications may be found on line at: *www.oecd.org/about/publishing/corrigenda.htm*.

Foreword

Agriculture is a provider of commodities such as food, feed, fibre and fuel and, it can also bring both positive and negative impacts on the environment such as biodiversity, water and soil quality. These environmental externalities from agricultural activities may have characteristics of non-rivalry and non-excludability. When they have such characteristics, they are defined as agri-environmental public goods. Agri-environmental public goods need not necessarily be desirable; that is, they may cause harm and can be defined as agri-environmental "public bads".

Public goods and externalities: Agri-environmental policy measures in selected OECD countries aims to improve our understanding of the best policy measures to provide agri-environmental public goods and reduce agri-environmental public bads, by looking at the experiences of the five OECD countries. It addresses a number of questions, including: How do these countries define agri-environmental public goods? How do they set agri-environmental targets and reference levels? Which policies do they implement and for which agri-environmental public goods? This book provides information to contribute to policy design addressing the provision of agri-environmental public goods including the reduction of agri-environmental public bads.

This book synthesises the five country papers prepared as background reports and published in the *OECD Food, Agriculture and Fisheries Paper* series:

- Public Goods and Externalities: Agri-environmental Policy Measures in Australia
- Public Goods and Externalities: Agri-environmental Policy Measures in Japan
- Public Goods and Externalities: Agri-environmental Policy Measures in the Netherlands
- Public Goods and Externalities: Agri-environmental Policy Measures in the United Kingdom
- Public Goods and Externalities: Agri-environmental Policy Measures in the United States

These five country papers are available free of charge on OECD iLibrary.

At their meeting in 2010, Agriculture Ministers requested the OECD to "identify policy options and market approaches that allow the incentives faced by farmers, the agro-food sector and consumers to better reflect underlying social and environmental costs and benefits, including with respect to public and private goods and services of agriculture." In 2011, at the OECD workshop on the evaluation of agri-environmental policies held in Braunschweig, Germany, it was acknowledged that further analysis of the cost-effectiveness of agri-environmental policies for public goods is necessary.

The OECD has undertaken a series of studies on agri-environmental public goods. Early work in this field focused on the conceptual questions arising from positive and negative environmental externalities associated with agricultural production. The *Guidelines for Cost-effective Agri-*environmental *Policy Measures* (*Guidelines*) synthesises previous conceptual work and identified the characteristics of a range of policy instruments addressing agri-environmental issues. In 2013, the study *Providing Agri-environmental Public Goods through Collective Action* focused on how farmers undertake collective action with other farmers and non-farmers to provide agri-environmental public goods. These studies clarified the general characteristics of diverse agri-environmental policy measures (agri-environmental payments, regulations, tradeable credits, etc.).

The OECD has also monitored and evaluated agricultural policies in OECD countries, including agri-environmental policies. The 2010 OECD report *Policy Measures Addressing Agri-environmental*

Issues (*Inventory*) focused on developments of the overall range of policies addressing environmental issues in agriculture in OECD countries since the mid-1990s. Other studies also provide numerous policy implications and country lessons. However, it remains unclear how each OECD country defines agri-environmental public goods and sets agri-environmental targets and reference levels, and what policies are implemented for targeting which agri-environmental public goods. These points have not been fully examined in OECD studies.

This project was carried out under the auspices of the OECD Joint Working Party on Agriculture and the Environment (JWPAE), of the Committee for Agriculture and the Environment Policy Committee. The JWPAE endorsed the report for declassification in June 2014.

The author is Tetsuya Uetake, Agricultural Policy Analyst in the Environment Division of the Trade and Agriculture Directorate.

Several experts contributed to the country case studies: James Jones (Cumulus Consultants Ltd., United Kingdom), David Pannell (University of Western Australia, Australia), Anna Roberts (Natural Decisions Pty Ltd, Australia), Raymond Schrijver (Wageningen UR Alterra Landscape Centre, Netherlands), James Shortle (Pennsylvania State University, United States) and Paul Silcock (Cumulus Consultants Ltd, United Kingdom).

Dimitris Diakosavvas, Guillaume Gruère, Franck Jesus, Hiroki Sasaki, and Vaclav Vojtech made valuable comments. Dale Andrew provided overall guidance. The manuscript was prepared for publication by Françoise Bénicourt, Michèle Patterson and Theresa Poincet.

Table of contents

Tables

Figures

Executive summary

This book aims to improve an understanding of the best policy measures to provide agri-environmental public goods and reduce agri-environmental public bads by looking at the experiences of five OECD countries: Australia, Japan, the Netherlands, the United Kingdom and the United States. A number of questions will be addressed, including: How do these countries define agri-environmental public goods? How do they set agri-environmental targets and reference levels? Which policies do they implement and for which agri-environmental public goods?

Targeted agri-environmental public goods and their priorities vary depending on the country because of, for example, history, culture, climate, and farm systems. Five agri-environmental public goods (soil protection and quality, water quality, water quantity and availability, air quality and biodiversity) are targeted in all the studied countries. Climate change (greenhouse gas emissions and carbon storage) is a targeted agri-environmental public good except in the United States. Agricultural landscapes are targeted agri-environmental public goods except in Australia. Resilience to natural disasters such as flooding and fire are targeted agri-environmental public goods in Japan, the Netherlands and the United Kingdom, but not in Australia and the United States.

Farmers form the largest group of natural resource managers in the world. Farm systems, inputs and practices and agricultural infrastructure (driving forces) affect the provision of agri-environmental public goods (environmental outcomes). Most policy measures target these driving forces, but performance-based policy measures, which target environmental outcomes, are few. Generally speaking, it is easier to target driving forces than outcomes because various factors, including non-agricultural ones, affect the environmental outcomes. Sometimes, targeting driving forces is the only practical option. In addition to policy design and methodological issues, countries also face challenges in obtaining appropriate data and linking environmental outputs to driving forces that policy measures often target.

Farmers can provide agri-environmental public goods without government intervention, and the supply may meet demand. It has been rarely examined, however, as to whether the supply in fact meets demand, although the case study countries have been trying to collect better data on both the demand and supply of agri-environmental public goods. This suggests that governments may intervene in cases where the supply does meet the demand and there are no market failures. There are risks of over-intervention. Where market failure exists, there are cases of insufficient or poor government intervention because of lack of information concerning the extent of market failure.

Cost-benefit analyses generally have not been undertaken due to technical difficulties. Some studies indicate there are cases where the costs of government intervention outweigh the benefits. At present, governments are trying to improve the cost-effectiveness of policy measures.

Environmental targets and reference levels are useful to discuss who should bear the costs for providing agri-environmental public goods, but they are not clearly defined or quantified in most cases. Many financial incentives set reference levels based on current farming practices so that governments are required to pay farmers to adopt sustainable farming practices. In some cases, direct beneficiaries of agri-environmental public goods can be identified. In this case, beneficiaries can bear some of the costs for its provision, thereby reducing the costs of government intervention as well as the farmer's burden. Community-based approaches or collective action can help and such organisations should be included in the discussion of the distribution of burdens.

Many policy measures (especially financial incentives such as agri-environmental payments) target multiple agri-environmental public goods, and each agri-environmental public good is targeted by multiple policy measures. It is not always clear to what extent a particular policy measure tries to address agri-environmental issues, and to what extent others do so.

Policy measures are complex because of the history of policy development and the involvement of multiple actors (e.g. ministries, central and local governments, stakeholders). Discussion on best policy mixes and co-ordination among actors is still inadequate.

Key recommendations

- Identify environmental externalities from agricultural activities that are important to countries and regions. Ensure that they have the characteristics of non-rivalry and non-excludability, and can be defined as agri-environmental public goods and not as private goods.
- Examine how agriculture can provide agri-environmental public goods, and foster knowledge-building and data-gathering.
- Pay greater attention to analysing demand and supply of agri-environmental public goods. Agri-environmental public goods can be local, regional or global public goods – thus, the examination of market failures associated with agriculture must be done at the appropriate scale.
- Identify to what extent farmers can voluntarily provide agri-environmental public goods without government intervention. Avoid paying farmers who would have improved their environmental performance without government payment, and pay attention to the additionality of a policy measure.
- Take a more rigorous approach in evaluating the benefits and costs of specific policy interventions – and also of non-intervention. Those benefits, to the extent possible, must be evaluated on the basis of the environmental outcomes and not according to the use of particular practices.
- Clearly and appropriately defined reference levels and environmental targets need to be established, and decisions on who bears what share of the costs (farmers, taxpayers, and consumers) should be made, prior to any government intervention.
- Target factors that affect the provision of agri-environmental public goods so as to improve the cost-effectiveness of policy measures. To improve the effectiveness of policy measures, take into account the heterogeneity of farmers and farmland characteristics, target related geographical areas, specific farm types, inputs, practices and infrastructure, and clearly define specific environmental objectives.
- Pay more attention to a wider range of motivations for farmers' actions concerning the environment. Farmers have different perceptions of environmental issues and their preferences and degree of compliance with policy measures differ among them. More research on farmer behaviour is necessary to develop a holistic approach towards agri-environmental public goods.
- Examine innovative approaches, such as auction systems based on environmental outcomes and payments for ecosystem services, undertaken by local governments and private companies. Learn from them to improve the cost-effectiveness of agri-environmental policies.
- Policy makers should choose the appropriate policy instruments by evaluating the trade-offs between environmental effectiveness, economic efficiency, administrative costs and constraints, and other benefits and costs, including consideration of equity and income distribution.
- Develop good policy mixes in order to provide agri-environmental public goods in a cost-effective way. Reviewing current policy measures and examining whether policy measures are not conflicting but creating synergies and bringing additionality is a first step.

Chapter 1

Agri-environmental public goods and externalities

This introductory chapter presents the key questions on which this report focuses, and the methodology used to analyse agri-environmental public goods and externalities. It then explains the theoretical background behind the analysis of agri-environmental public goods. This book defines agri-environmental public goods as those environmental externalities from agricultural activities that have the characteristics of non-excludability and non-rivalry.

Introduction

Agriculture is a provider of commodities such as food, feed, fibre and fuel and, it can also bring both positive and negative impacts on the environment such as biodiversity, water and soil quality. Some of these public goods tend to be local (e.g. agricultural landscapes) while others may be global (e.g. carbon storage). The OECD study on agri-environmental indicators (OECD, 2013a) identified that environmental performance of agriculture has improved in some areas, such as nutrients, pesticides, energy and water management. However, it also showed that such progress in several regions in OECD countries has been limited, and that addressing the challenges to ensure global food security and improve environmental performance will require more efforts from farmers, policy makers and the agro-food chain.

Objectives

This publication will examine the following key questions by synthesising selected country experiences.

- How do countries define agri-environmental public goods?
- How are agri-environmental public goods provided by farmers?
- How do countries estimate demand and supply of agri-environmental public goods? Does the incidental provision of agri-environmental public goods meet demand? Have countries examined whether market failures associated with the agri-environmental public goods exist?
- Where there are market failures associated with the agri-environmental public goods, who should bear the costs of providing them? How do countries set agri-environmental targets and reference levels; and
- What policies are implemented to provide agri-environmental public goods and what agri-environmental public goods are targeted by which policy measures?

The main objectives here are twofold: to provide a link between previous conceptual OECD studies (e.g. *Guidelines*) and OECD country policies, and to contribute to a better understanding of good policy measures for agri-environmental public goods. This publication is one of the first to apply conceptual frameworks (e.g. the reference level framework) established by previous OECD studies to selected OECD countries and to compares experiences. In addition, it examines how policy measures target agri-environmental public goods in selected OECD countries, and contributes to policy design for good policy measures and policy mixes for agri-environmental public goods.

Methodologies

To analyse the main issues, the experiences on policy measures for agri-environmental public goods of selected countries are examined via a literature review and country case studies. Analysis is also based on information provided by OECD governments, experts in the field, and other sources, e.g. academic literature, books and the internet.

Case studies review the experiences of five selected OECD countries: Australia, Japan, the Netherlands, the United Kingdom and the United States. The countries were selected to ensure that all world regions (Asia and Oceania, Europe, and North America) were covered, thus making it possible to cover agricultural management systems and policy measures in different regions, and to examine various agri-environmental public goods, agricultural management systems, and policy measures.

This book synthesises findings from the case studies and the literature review. However, it should be noted that because of the limited number of countries covered, the coverage of policy measures for agri-environmental public goods is limited and cannot be generally applied to all OECD countries.

Theoretical framework of agri-environmental public goods

Agriculture can bring both positive and negative impacts on the environment, and these environmental externalities from agricultural activities may also have characteristics of non-rivalry and non-excludability (OECD, 1999, 2013b). When goods satisfy the two criteria of being non-excludable and non-rival, they are defined as public goods (Samuelson, 1954; 1955).

- Non-excludability: The nature of the good is such that it is impossible to exclude anyone from consuming it.
- Non-rivalry: The same good can be consumed by anyone without diminishing the consumption opportunities available to others.

Environmental externalities from agricultural activities can be classified into four types of goods: pure public goods, common pool resources (CPRs), club goods and private goods, depending on the degree of non-rivalry and non-excludability.

Table 1.1. Classification of agri-environmental public goods[1, 2]

		Rivalry (subtractability)	
		Low	High
Excludability	Difficult	*Pure public goods* • Biodiversity (non-use value[5]) • Agricultural landscapes (non-use value) • Flood control • Landslide prevention	*Common pool resources*[3] • Biodiversity (use-value[4]) • Water quantity/availability
		Agri-environmental public goods	
	Easy	*Club goods* • Biodiversity (if exclusive to club members)	*Private goods* • Agricultural commodities • Agricultural landscape (use value by visitors if exclusion can be made)

1. The list given in each cell is not exhaustive, but covers some of the main examples. Depending on the situation, the same goods can be private goods (rival and excludable) or public goods and when they cause harm, they can be defined as private bads or public bads (Kolstad, 2011). Thus careful examination is necessary for each case and each situation.
2. Targeted agri-environmental public goods in the case study countries are explained in Chapter 2. Box 2.1 provides additional information on each public good.
3. CPRs offer non-rival benefits until saturation or congestion point is reached. After that point, their services are highly rival.
4. Use-value: Value representing i) the value associated with actual use and ii) the value of having the ability to make choices in an uncertain future (option value).
5. Non-use value: Value representing i) the value that humans attach to the simple fact of a resource's existence and ii) the value that humans attach to the possibility of maintaining a resource for future generations.

Source: Adapted from OECD (2013b), *Providing Agri-environmental Public goods through Collective Action*, based on OECD (2001), *Multifunctionality: Towards an Analytical Framework*, and C. Hess and E. Ostrom (eds.) (2007), *Understanding Knowledge as a Commons: From Theory to Practice*.

Some environmental externalities from agricultural activities can be treated as private goods. In this case, government direct intervention may not be necessary. For example, where agricultural landscapes are exclusive to visitors, these visitors may be able to cover the costs for the provision of the agricultural landscapes (OECD, 2005). Therefore, environmental externalities from agricultural activities that have the characteristics of public goods (including impure public goods), in this book, defined as *agri-environmental public goods*, become issues of agri-environmental policies. Table 1.1 gives examples of agri-environmental public goods.

Box 1.1. Theories of externalities and public goods

Externalities

Externalities occur when decisions about production or consumption by one person affect someone else without this being taken into account by the decision maker. If one person's action has a positive impact on another, the externality is defined as positive. A classic example of a positive externality is an agricultural example, where a beekeeper benefits neighbouring farmers by supplying pollination services as an unintended effect of his/her production of honey, and from which the farmers' crops benefits. Another example of a positive externality is the grazing of animals on pasture. Many people enjoy seeing these animals and consider that they enhance the agricultural landscape. However, when and how long they graze is decided by the farmer as part of his/her production plan (OECD, 2013b).

When the externality decreases the well-being or utility of the affected person, it is defined as a negative externality. A typical example of a negative externality is pollution. Agriculture produces negative externalities such as water pollution and soil erosion as a result of the use of fertilisers and pesticides, or unsustainable farming methods (OECD, 2013b).

Public goods

Pure public goods are goods that satisfy the two criteria of being non-excludable and non-rival (Samuelson, 1954; 1955). In reality, few products fully meet both these criteria, whereas a number of goods are *only to a certain extent* excludable and/or rival (Cooper et al., 2009; OECD, 2013b). Goods that are neither private goods (i.e. fully rival and excludable goods) nor pure public goods (i.e. fully non-rival and non-excludable goods) are called impure public goods. They can be further sub-divided into two main groups, common pool resources (CPRs) and club goods, according to the degree of their excludability and rivalry.

Many environmental externalities from agricultural activities also have characteristics of non-rivalry and/or non-excludability. Thus, environmental externalities from agriculture are, in many cases, also public goods (either pure public goods, CPRs or club goods) (OECD, 1999, 2013b; Kolstad, 2011; Laffont, 1988), but not all externalities are public goods because some of them can be private goods (Dwyer and Guyomard, 2006).

For private goods, prices tell market participants how valuable one good is, and prices tell producers how much they should produce to maximise their benefits. Some environmental externalities from agricultural activities can be treated as private goods. In this case, direct government intervention might not be necessary. For example, if certain agricultural landscapes are exclusive to visitors, visitors may be able to cover the costs of the provision of the agricultural landscapes (OECD, 2005).

Pure public goods

The provision of pure public goods poses a free rider problem: providers of pure public goods cannot exclude anyone who tries to enjoy the benefits without paying for them, thus making it difficult for individuals to provide pure public goods on a commercial basis. Although the market may very well provide some public goods, in many cases, it under-provides public goods (Kolstad, 2011). Therefore, governments generally play an important role in their provision (OECD, 2013b).
Common pool resources

CPRs are goods which are rival (subtractable) but for which it is difficult to exclude someone from consuming them. This leads to a risk of overexploitation. This situation is known as "the tragedy of the commons" (see, for example, Hardin, 1968). A shared pasture, for example, would be depleted if each herder put a maximum number of cows on the land (OECD, 2013b). In this case, to prevent this over-exploitation, the role of government could be to facilitate discussions among community members and help them to successfully regulate CPRs by setting up community rules (OECD, 2003, 2013b). If property rights are successfully established and are exclusive to members, CPRs could be treated as a club good. For example, in France, there are communal hunting associations and hunting companies that manage CPRs effectively by transforming them into club goods. Negotiations amongst these different associations have limited hunting in France solely to their members.

Where CPRs are not owned by anyone, they are sometimes called "open access resources" since it is hard to prevent free access to resources due to the lack of exclusionary systems.

Club goods

Non-members are excluded from consuming club goods. In contrast, members may consume the goods without rivalry, unless there is a risk of overcrowding or deterioration of the good. An example of a club good is the protection of wildlife on a certain tract of land, or of fish stocks in a watercourse, paid for by syndicates of hunters who have exclusive hunting rights in the areas concerned, and prevent others from enjoying the wildlife, either for hunting or simply for the pleasure of observing it. In this case, governments could play a role in establishing the institutional infrastructure to encourage club creation by, for example, defining property rights that enable clubs to charge their members, by establishing institutional frameworks by which non-profit organisations can work effectively, by preparing regulatory frameworks, and by providing knowledge (OECD, 2003; 2013b).

The term "toll good" is also used for excludable and non-rival goods because the term "club good" can be misleading for some excludable and non-rival goods, such as toll roads. Although users pay fees to use toll roads (i.e. they can be made excludable), these users are not club members of toll roads. A national park can also be an example of a toll good if people are required to pay an entrance fee.

Box 1.1. Theories of externalities and public goods (*cont.*)

Pure public goods and impure public goods will need different degrees of government intervention. For instance, CPRs may need to create rules to manage resources, and governments can provide technical information and assistance. Club goods may need institutional assistance and legislation for creating clubs. On the other hand, pure public goods may need agri-environmental payments (OECD, 2003; 2005; 2013b).

Public bads

Public goods need not necessarily be desirable; that is, they may cause harm (OECD, 1992; Mas-Colell et al., 1995). If non-rival and non-excludable goods cause harm and people do not want them, the term, *public bads*, may be used (Mas-Colell et al., 1995; Dwyer and Guyomard, 2006; Kolstad, 2011). In this case, non-excludability means it is impossible to exclude anyone from avoiding the consumption of the bad, and non-rivalry means the same bad can be consumed by anyone without diminishing the consumption opportunities available to others. There are impure public bads as well, depending on the degree of non-rivalry and non-excludability (Kolstad, 2011).

The Pareto optimal provision of the public bad is that the marginal damage to each individual consumer should be summed over the population and equated to the marginal cost of pollution abatement (Kolstad, 2011). Agriculture produces agri-environmental public bads, and reducing the supply of agri-environmental public bads so as to correspond to the socially demanded level is an important policy challenge.

For a given goal or objective, a "benefit" is the result of an action that leads to an environmental outcome beyond a certain environmental level, while a "harm" is the result of an action that leads to an environmental outcome below that level. An environmental benefit (or harm) has to be viewed as relative to a certain environmental level (OECD, 1997), and this environmental level can vary depending on the country and the local situation.

Public goods, however, need not necessarily be desirable; that is, they may cause harm (OECD, 1992; Mas-Colell et al., 1995). If non-rival and non-excludable goods cause harm and people do not want them, the term, *public bads*, may be used (Mas-Colell et al., 1995; Dwyer and Guyomard, 2006; Kolstad, 2011). Agriculture produces agri-environmental public bads, and reducing the supply of agri-environmental public bads so as to correspond to the socially demanded level is an important policy challenge.

Although this theoretical classification of public goods (and public bads) is useful, it is necessary to understand which agri-environmental public goods are provided (and agri-environmental public bads are reduced) in each country in order to develop agri-environmental policy measures. This is because countries may have different perceptions about what a public good (and a public bad) is, and its relative importance may also differ among OECD countries (OECD, 2012). Chapters 2 to 5 will examine these points by synthesising the experiences of agri-environmental public goods and policies in the five countries under study. Box 1.1 provides more theoretical explanation on public goods and externalities.

References

Cooper, T., K. Hart and D. Baldock (2009), *The Provision of Public Goods through Agriculture in the European Union*, report prepared for DG Agriculture and Rural Development, Contract No 30-CE-023309/00-28, Institute for European Environmental Policy, London.

Dwyer, J. and H. Guyomard (2006), "International Trade, Agricultural Policy Reform and the Multifunctionality of EU Agriculture: A Framework for Analysis," in *Trade Agreements, Multifunctionality and EU Agriculture*, Centre for European Policy Studies, Brussels.

Hardin, G. (1968), "The Tragedy of the Commons," *Science*, Vol. 162, pp. 1243-1248, http://www.sciencemag.org/content/162/3859/1243.full.

Hess, C. and E. Ostrom (eds.) (2007), *Understanding Knowledge as a Commons: From Theory to Practice*, MIT Press, Cambridge.

Jones, J., P. Silcock and T. Uetake (2015), "Public Goods and Externalities: Agri-environmental Policy Measures in the United Kingdom", *OECD Food, Agriculture and Fisheries Papers*, No. 83, OECD Publishing, Paris.
DOI: http://dx.doi.org/10.1787/5js08hw4drd1-en

Kolstad, C.D. (2011), *Intermediate Environmental Economics: International Second Edition*, Oxford University Press, New York.

Laffont, J.J. (1988), *Fundamentals of Public Economics*, The Massachusetts Institute of Technology, Cambridge.

Mas-Colell, A., M.D. Whinston and J.R. Green (1995), *Microeconomic Theory*, Oxford University Press Inc., Oxford.

OECD (2013a), *OECD Compendium of Agri-environmental Indicators*, OECD Publishing, Paris.
DOI: http://dx.doi.org/10.1787/9789264186217-en.

OECD (2013b), *Providing Agri-environmental Public Goods through Collective Action*, OECD Publishing, Paris.
DOI: http://dx.doi.org/10.1787/9789264197213-en.

OECD (2012), *Evaluation of Agri-environmental Policies: Selected Methodological Issues and Case Studies*, OECD Publishing, Paris.
DOI: http://dx.doi.org/10.1787/9789264179332-en.

OECD (2005), *Multifunctionality in Agriculture: What Role for Private Initiatives?*, OECD Publishing, Paris.
DOI: http://dx.doi.org/10.1787/9789264014473-en.

OECD (2003), *Multifunctionality: The Policy Implications*, OECD Publishing, Paris.
DOI: http://dx.doi.org/10.1787/9789264104532-en.

OECD (2001), *Multifunctionality: Towards an Analytical Framework*, OECD Publishing, Paris.
DOI: http://dx.doi.org/10.1787/9789264192171-en.

OECD (1999), *Cultivating Rural Amenities: An Economic Development Perspective*, OECD Publishing, Paris.
DOI: http://dx.doi.org/10.1787/9789264173941-en.

OECD (1997), "Environmental Benefits from Agriculture: Issues and Policies", OECD General distribution document, Paris.

OECD (1992), *Agricultural Policy Reform and Public Goods*, OECD Publishing, Paris.

Pannell, D. and A. Roberts (2015), "Public goods and externalities: agri-environmental policy measures in Australia", *OECD Food, Agriculture and Fisheries Papers*, No. 80, OECD Publishing, Paris.
DOI: http://dx.doi.org/10.1787/5js08hx1btlw-en

Samuelson, P.A. (1955), "Diagrammatic Exposition of a Theory of Public Expenditure", *Review of Economics and Statistics*, Vol. 37, pp. 350-356, https://courses.cit.cornell.edu/econ335/out/samuelson_diag.pdf.

Samuelson, P.A. (1954), "The Pure Theory of Public Expenditure", *Review of Economics and Statistics*, Vol. 36, pp. 387-389, http://www.ses.unam.mx/docencia/2007II/Lecturas/Mod3_Samuelson.pdf.

Schrijver, R. and T. Uetake (2015), "Public goods and externalities: agri-environmental policy measures in the Netherlands", *OECD Food, Agriculture and Fisheries Papers*, No. 82, OECD Publishing, Paris.
DOI: http://dx.doi.org/10.1787/5js08hwpr1q8-en

Shortle, J. and T. Uetake (2015), "Public Goods and Externalities: Agri-environmental Policy Measures in the the United States", *OECD Food, Agriculture and Fisheries Papers*, No. 84, OECD Publishing, Paris.
DOI: http://dx.doi.org/10.1787/5js08hwhg8mw-en

Uetake, T. (2015), "Public goods and externalities: agri-environmental policy measures in Japan", *OECD Food, Agriculture and Fisheries Papers*, No. 81, OECD Publishing, Paris.
DOI: http://dx.doi.org/10.1787/5js08hwsjj26-en

Chapter 2

Main agri-environmental public goods and their provision through farming practice

This chapter examines how countries variously define agri-environmental public goods and how this affects the choice of policies that target these public goods. It also examines how agri-environmental public goods are provided by farmers. Various driving forces (farm systems, farming practices, farm inputs and agricultural infrastructure) affect environmental outcomes (the provision of agri-environmental public goods). Some farming practices and policy measures bring both positive and negative impacts on the agri-environmental public goods in a different way and degree. This chapter shows the importance of how a better understanding of agriculture can provide agri-environmental public goods.

Overview of the main agri-environmental public goods

Table 2.1 summarises the agri-environmental public goods (and public bads) that are targeted in Australia, Japan, the Netherlands, the United Kingdom and the United States.[1, 2] Information about these goods is provided in Box 2.1.

Table 2.1. Agri-environmental public goods targeted in several OECD countries[1, 2]

	Australia	Japan	Netherlands	United Kingdom	United States
Soil protection and quality	XX	X	X	XX	XX
Water quality	XX	X	XX	XXX	XXX
Water quantity/availability	XXX	XX	X	X	X
Air quality	X	X	XX	XX	X
Climate change – greenhouse gas emissions	X	XX	XX	XX	NA
Climate change – carbon storage	X	X	XX	XX	NA
Biodiversity	XXX[4]	XX	XXX	XXX	XXX[5]
Agricultural landscapes	NA	XX	XXX	XXX	X
Resilience to natural disasters[3]	NA	XXX	XX	X	NA

1. NA – not applied or marginal; X – low importance; XX – medium importance; XXX – high importance. The importance of the agri-environmental public goods is related to the priorities of the specific country. It is not designed to compare the importance of specific agri-environmental public goods across countries.
2. As explained in Chapter 1, these goods are not always public goods. Sometimes, they can be private goods (e.g. agricultural landscape with use value by visitors can be a private good if exclusion can be made) or when they cause harm, they can be defined as private bads or public bads (Kolstad, 2011). Careful examination on whether these goods have characteristics of non-rivalry and/or non-excludability is necessary for each case.
3. Resilience to natural disasters includes resilience to flooding, fire, snow damage and landslide.
4. In Australia, the focus on biodiversity is on native vegetation that is on farms but not part of the agricultural production system (Pannell and Roberts, 2015).
5. In the United States, the focus on biodiversity is on protection of wetlands and wildlife habitat (Shortle and Uetake, 2015).

Source: OECD Secretariat based on Pannell, D. and A. Roberts (2015), *Public Goods and Externalities: Agri-environmental Policy Measures in Australia*, Uetake, T. (2015), *Public Goods and Externalities: Agri-environmental Policy Measures in Japan*, Schrijver and Uetake (2015), *Public Goods and Externalities: Agri-environmental Policy Measures in the Netherlands*, Jones et al., (2015), *Public Goods and Externalities: Agri-environmental Policy Measures in the United Kingdom*, and Shortle and Uetake (2015), *Public Goods and Externalities: Agri-environmental Policy Measures in the United States.*

In Vojtech (2010), soil protection and quality, water quality, air quality, climate change (greenhouse gas mitigation), biodiversity and agricultural landscape are identified as agri-environmental public goods (and public bads). However, it is clear that others, i.e. water availability, carbon storage, and resilience to natural disasters, are also targeted in several OECD countries.

The domain of agri-environmental public goods (and public bads) varies according to the public concern and the development of policy measures. Agri-environmental policies began when public demand for environmental protection emerged and people recognised that agricultural practices could pose environmental risks. When it became evident that the quality of soil, water and air was affected by agricultural pollution this became a public policy issue. For example, the 1930s "Dust Bowl" in the Great Plains of the United States and Canada led to the development of an array of soil quality programmes (Shortle and Uetake, 2015). Other issues have since arose, such as biodiversity and climate change, and more recently there is growing interest in carbon storage, particularly following the release of the Intergovernmental Panel on Climate Change (IPCC) report in 2007, which stated that carbon storage could greatly contribute to climate change mitigation (IPCC, 2007).

Public concerns and perceptions about agriculture and the environment differ among OECD countries so that the targeted agri-environmental public goods (and public bads) are also different. In the United States, for example, greenhouse gas (GHG) emissions recently became a target of federal regulatory measures, although agriculture does not yet have targets set to limit GHG emissions programmes. Carbon storage is also of considerable policy interest but not yet an area of significant policy development (Shortle and Uetake, 2015).

The farming system of the case study countries is related to targeted agri-environmental public goods (and public bads). Since paddy fields constitute the main type of farmland in Japan, agri-environmental public goods associated with paddy fields are important for Japan, but not for the other four countries. Paddy fields and their irrigation systems prevent some natural disasters by retaining water (resilience to flooding) and providing water for extinguishing fire (resilience to fire) and melting snow (resilience to snow damage) (Uetake, 2015). Prevention of natural disasters is also regarded as an agri-environmental public good in the United Kingdom and the Netherlands. Some flooding and fires are prevented by good grazing management and, in the United Kingdom, this contributes to improved soil permeability and water storage (Jones et al., 2015). In the Netherlands, flooding risks are reduced by the water retention capacity of the agricultural areas by controlling the level of water tables (Schrijver and Uetake, 2015).

Local public goods and global public goods

The spatial scales of many agri-environmental public goods (and public bads) have expanded from local public goods to global public goods. Figure 2.1 illustrates the targeted agri-environmental public goods in the case study countries and their spatial scale in a highly stylised form. Most of the original targeted agri-environmental public goods, i.e. soil, water and air quality, are local public goods, while the recently targeted agri-environmental public goods, i.e. biodiversity and climate change, are global public goods. Kerkhof et al. (2010) reviewed 117 environmental case studies and classified them at the local, landscape/watershed, regional, or global levels. It also identified that the majority of studies are related to the local and landscape/watershed levels, but that the number of cases at the regional and global levels has been increasing.

Figure 2.1. Agri-environmental public goods and spatial scale

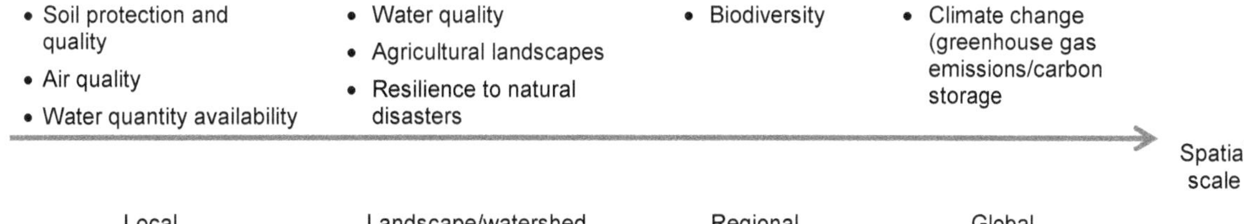

1. This figure is a simplified illustration. Agri-environmental public goods (and public bads) do not always belong to each category of the spatial scale. Spatial scales vary depending on actual situations.

Source: OECD Secretariat based on Kerkhof, A., et al. (2010), "Valuation of Environmental Public Goods and Services at Different Spatial Scales: A Review", *Journal of Integrative Environmental Sciences*.

Local and global public goods (and public bads) need different approaches. Regarding local public goods, it may be easier to identify producers of agri-environmental public goods and its consumers and develop solutions to overcome market failures through negotiations between them. For example, if farmers pollute local water courses or produce odours, negotiations between farmers and local communities may be able to improve water and air quality. On the other hand, direct negotiations are difficult for global public goods such as greenhouse gas emission and carbon sequestration. The supply of these goods depends on highly heterogeneous local conditions, while their demand is global.

Spatial scale and excludability are also related. In general, it is difficult to establish exclusion systems when the spatial scale increases, which suggests that global public goods tend to be pure public goods. Hereinafter, the term *agri-environmental public goods* is used for externalities associated with agriculture that have characteristics of non-rivalry and/or non-excludability.[3]

Box 2.1. Main characteristics of agri-environmental public goods

Nine agri-environmental public goods are targeted in the OECD case study countries studies (although not all agri-environmental public goods are targeted by all countries studied): soil protection and quality, water quality, water quantity/availability, air quality, climate change (carbon storage and greenhouse gas emissions), biodiversity, agricultural landscapes, and resilience to natural disasters (e.g. flooding, fire).

Some agri-environmental public goods are inter-connected. For example, good soil quality can enhance the capacity to provide biodiversity, water and air quality, and carbon storage. Good water quality is also beneficial to biodiversity and landscapes.

Since these goods are not always public goods, careful examination on whether these goods have characteristics of non-rivalry and/or non-excludability is necessary for each case. Sometimes, they can be private goods (e.g. agricultural landscape with use value by visitors can be a private good if exclusion can be enforced). This box provides a brief explanation on the main general characteristics of these agri-environmental public goods.

Soil protection and quality

Agriculture impacts on soil quality and soil functionality since most agriculture relies its production on the soil. Soil organic matter content and soil contamination are the main issues of soil quality. Excessive or inadequate applications of pesticides and fertilisers deteriorate soil quality and have risks to human health as well, while it can be improved by adapting appropriate management practices (Vojtech, 2010).

In many OECD countries, soil erosion is also a main environmental issue associated with agriculture (Vojtech, 2010; OECD, 2013). The soil erosion risk comes from natural forces (water erosion, wind erosion) and from soil cultivation practices (e.g. cultivation of fragile soils, overgrazing) (Vojtech, 2010). Soil erosion is primary addressed by good farming practices such as transfers of arable land to grassland, extensive use of pastures, green cover, or no-tillage or low-tillage practices (Vojtech, 2010; OECD, 2013). Soil quality is judged by the number of indicators such as the proportion of organic matter, the level of susceptibility to erosion, the soil structure and capacity for infiltration, the health of its biota and its level of contamination (Cooper et al., 2009).

Soil has the characteristics of both a private and public good, thus careful examination of characteristics of public goods is necessary. Soil is under private control and enhancing its quality brings private benefits to farmers. Usually, these private benefits belong exclusively to farmers but good soil can cause rivalry and thus it is a private good.

However, farmers have a short-term incentive to maximise productivity through the heavy use of pesticides and fertilisers or inappropriate farming practice, which can result in the undersupply of soil quality and deplete soil functionality for the future (Cooper et al., 2009). Sometimes, these public goods are called intertemporal public goods (Gerber and Wichardt, 2013). In addition, preventing soil pollution and contamination and soil erosion is important not only for the environment, but also for human health. Moreover, soil conservation brings various off-farm benefits such as biodiversity, water and air quality, and carbon storage. These future values, off-farm impacts of soil quality and soil-related values can be non-excludable and non-rival. Thus, although soil is a private land owned and managed by farmers, its protection and quality for the present and the future is a public interest and it can be public goods, depending on the situation.

Water quality

Agriculture has impacts on water quality. Farming practices and farm inputs can deteriorate water quality through various pollutants including sediment, nutrients and pathogens (Ribaudo et al., 2008). One of the features of water pollution originated from agriculture is that pollution from farmers spread across the landscape (diffuse source pollution), as opposed to more spatially confined sources such as urban centres (point source pollution). Intensive livestock farms, however, can be a point source of water pollution (OECD, 2013). Water quality issues include, for instance, salinity and eutrophication, and water pollution are typically non-rival and non-excludable.

Box 2.1. Main characteristics of agri-environmental public goods (*cont.*)

Farmers can improve water quality by adopting good farming practices which reduce the discharge of nutrients, pesticides, sediment, and other agricultural pollutants to water resources (Ribaudo et al., 2008). Clean water is vital in securing economic benefits for agriculture and other sectors, meeting human health needs, maintaining viable ecosystems, and providing societal benefits such as recreational and cultural values society attaches to water systems (OECD, 2012; 2013). Benefits from water quality can be non-rival and non-excludable.

Water quantity/availability

Agriculture is one of the largest users of water (OECD, 2010a; 2013). Agriculture accounts for 44% of total freshwater withdrawals (2008-10) in OECD countries. However, these shares vary considerably across countries: 66% in Japan; 52% in Australia, 40% in the United States, 15% in the United Kingdom and 1% in the Netherlands (OECD, 2013).

Water is a limited resource. It can be rivalry, although exclusion may be difficult (CPRs). To reduce future pressure on the demand for water and secure the continuous supply of water, promoting the efficient use of water by agriculture is important. For this purpose, in many OECD countries there are regulations to determine how much water is available to agriculture and how much must be retained for environmental purposes (Vojtech, 2010). This system can to a certain extent transform water resources to club goods (excludable and non-rival goods up to a certain point).

In addition to regulating water usage by agriculture, some countries try to enhance abilities of groundwater recharge by agriculture. For example, about 20% of groundwater is recharged by paddy fields in Japan (Mitsubishi Research Institute, 2001). Water used for paddy fields percolates through soils and becomes ground water and benefits society.

Air quality

Air quality is, normally, a public good, which can affect all of us (non-rival and non-excludable). Agriculture impacts on air quality by releasing a wide variety of material into the air, not only greenhouse gas, but also other materials such as ammonia, odours and pesticides (Ribaudo et al., 2008; OECD, 2013). Field operations produce windblown soil and pesticides while animal operations release ammonia and odours. These pollutants may affect people's health especially in densely populated areas and reduce visibility (Ribaudo et al., 2008). Agriculture can improve air quality by reducing the release of these materials through changing farming management practices (Ribaudo et al., 2008; Cooper et al., 2009).

Climate change

Although most air quality issue is a local issues (local public goods), climate change is an important global issue (global public goods) and it affects the entire universe (non-rival and non-excludable). Although agriculture is a net contributor of greenhouse gas emissions, a wide range of agricultural practices can promote carbon storage and reduce greenhouse gas (GHG) emissions.

Greenhouse gas emissions

GHG such as nitrous oxide (N_2O), methane (CH_4) and carbon dioxide (CO_2) are emitted through the use of inorganic fertilisers and manures, machinery and in livestock rearing. Overall, the share of agriculture in total OECD GHG emissions was 8% in 2008-10, but averaged much higher for nitrous oxide (N_2O) and methane (CH_4), at 75% and 38% respectively (OECD, 2013).

Farming practices such as changing livestock manure disposal methods, more timely and efficient use of fertilisers and soil tillage practices can lower GHGs emission rates per unit of output volume.

Carbon storage

Agriculture can sequester carbon in soils and offset GHG emissions. For sequestrating carbon in soils, it is important to minimise the rates of depletion of carbon from the soil, and enhance its absorption capacity (Cooper et al., 2009). The extent to which carbon can be stored depends on various factors including soil type, moisture conditions, vegetation patterns and cultivation practices (Trumper et al., 2009).

IPCC states that carbon storage can contribute to a large proportion of the climate change mitigation (IPCC, 2007). For example, some studies indicate huge amount of carbon can be annually stored in croplands and grazing lands through conservation tillage, crop rotations and fertilizer management (e.g. Lewandrowski et al., 2004). The recent OECD study on environmental co-benefits and stacking in environmental markets examines carbon policies (Lankoski, 2015).

Box 2.1. Main characteristics of agri-environmental public goods (*cont.*)

Biodiversity

Biodiversity is the variability among living organisms and the ecological complexes of which they are a part. Human intervention has significant impacts on biodiversity (Vojtech, 2010). Agricultural biodiversity is distinct in that it is largely created, maintained, and managed by humans through a range of farming systems from subsistence to those using a range of biotechnologies and extensively modified terrestrial ecosystems. In this regard, agricultural biodiversity stands in contrast to "wild" biodiversity which is most valued *in situ* and as a product of natural evolution (OECD, 2008; 2013). OECD (2013) defines agricultural biodiversity as follows:

- *Genetic diversity*: the number of genes within domesticated plants and livestock species and their wild relatives.
- *Species diversity*: the number and population of wild species (flora and fauna) both dependent on, or impacted by, agricultural activities, including soil biodiversity and effects of non-native species on agriculture and biodiversity.
- *Ecosystem diversity*: populations of domesticated and wild species and their non-living environment (e.g. climate), which make up an agro-ecosystem and which are in contact with other ecosystems (i.e. forest, aquatic, steppe, rocky and urban). The agro-ecosystem consists of a variety of habitats limited to an area where the ecological components are quite homogenous and are cultivated, such as extensive pasture or an orchard, or are uncultivated but within a farming system, such as a wetland.

Agricultural biodiversity has both use and non-use values. Although use values can be rival and excludable, its non-use values are non-rival and non-excludable, and thus can be public goods.

Because of the dominance of private farmland ownership, governments cannot do effective wildlife management without collaboration with farmers. OECD countries employ a variety of policies and approaches to reconcile the need of agricultural production, drawing on plant and livestock genetic resources, and yet reduce harmful biodiversity impacts (Vojtech, 2010).

Agricultural landscape

The long history of human and nature has created human-made agricultural landscapes, and which are highly appreciated in some countries. Their benefits are, in many cases, non-rival and non-excludable, although some agricultural landscapes can be exclusively provided to specific visitors who bear some costs (OECD, 2005). Its objectives can vary from site-specific to very generic ones, and are subject to various sets of policies. They are implemented mainly in Japan, the Netherlands and the United Kingdom, where the cultural landscape has been shaped by agriculture over many centuries, and it is becoming an environmental target in the United States as well. Elements of composing agricultural landscape include trees, hedges, stonewalls, ponds and marshes (Vojtech, 2010).

For instance, in Japan, the long-term relationship between human activities and agriculture has led to the development of *Satoyama* landscapes (Uetake, 2015). Agricultural landscapes and agricultural biodiversity are greatly appreciated in Japan. Some elements of Japanese biodiversity have developed as a result of human influence on natural environments, in addition to the untouched, natural environments. People have developed and maintained human-influenced natural environments sustainably over a long time (MOE and UNU-IAS, 2010). These natural environments are often called *Satoyama* landscapes. Among various types of farmlands, in Japan, paddy fields play a key role in providing landscapes and buffers for water flows, and in contributing to food security (OECD, 2010b). However, paddy fields have decreased continuously over the last 20 years, largely due to their conversion to non-agricultural use. To preserve *Satoyama* landscapes, the Japanese government launched the *Satoyama* Initiative.

Resilience to natural disasters

Some countries consider that appropriate management of agriculture provides resilience to natural disasters such as flooding, fire, snow damage and landslide. These benefits are usually non-rival and non-excludable, thus public goods (mostly local public goods at the landscape/watershed level). For instance, some farming practices can enhance flood control. Improving soil quality and structure can contribute to the improved infiltration rates. Irrigation systems, paddy fields and some land use choices such as the targeted creation of grass buffers, hedgerows or woodland strips can retain water and slow the passage of water (Cooper et al., 2009; Jones et al., 2015; Schrijver and Uetake, 2015; Uetake, 2015). In order to make the resilience effective, a majority of farmers at the catchment scale need to adopt necessary farming practices and maintain systems (OECD, 2005). This resilience to flooding is, in many cases, regarded as a public good in Japan, the Netherland and the United Kingdom.

There are many cases of fire, both natural and human-made ones. In some areas, certain farming practices such as making open patches or maintaining irrigation systems and paddy fields can create buffers to the fire and reduce the risk of its spreading over large areas of land. Improving resilience to fire is of public concern, thus, it is, in many cases, regarded as a public good in Japan and the United Kingdom (Jones et al., 2015; Uetake, 2015).

In addition, the irrigation canals of paddy fields in Japan can also be used to melt snow, which mitigates snow damages, and prevents landslides as the paddy fields can retain water. These benefits are non-excludable and non-rival and appreciated in some parts of Japan (local public goods) (Uetake, 2015).

Driving forces of agri-environmental public goods

Farmers are the largest group of natural resource managers in the world (FAO, 2007). Most of the provision of agri-environmental public goods is associated with certain agri-environmental systems or practices. Cooper et al. (2009) identify three main factors that affect the provision of public goods in the European Union, namely 1) certain agricultural systems (particularly extensive farming), 2) farming practices (e.g. reduction of inputs), and 3) agricultural infrastructure (e.g. drainage and irrigation). The OECD has explained the linkages between agricultural driving forces (e.g. farm systems, farm practices and farm input use) and the state of the environment (e.g. water quality, biodiversity) by using the Driving Force-State-Response Model (OECD, 2013). Whilst referring to these studies, Figure 2.2 depicts a simple relationship between agriculture and agri-environmental public goods (Figure 2.2).

Figure 2.2. Provision mechanisms of agri-environmental public goods

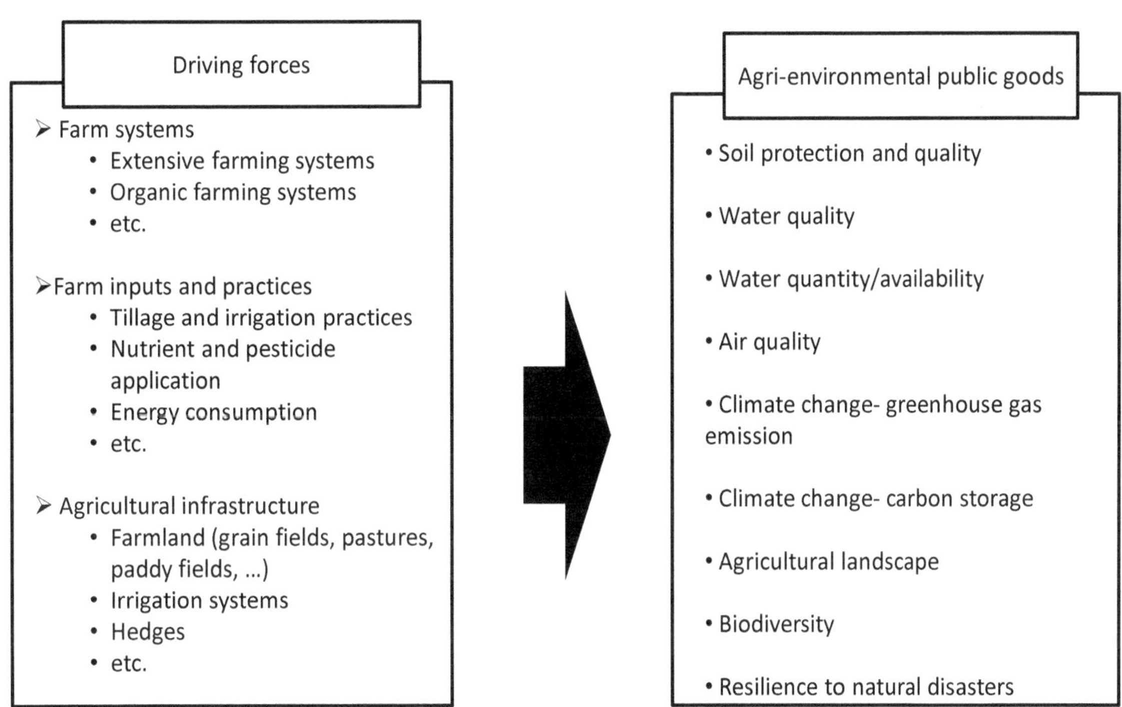

The provision of the agri-environmental public goods is affected by several driving forces: farm systems, farm inputs and practices, and agricultural infrastructure. The distinction between driving forces and agri-environmental public goods is important since broadly speaking, policy measures target drivers (*in-put based* or means) and agri-environmental public goods (*output-based* or ends) (OECD, 2010c).[4]

It is important to collect relevant data for the better understanding of the relationship between driving forces and agri-environmental public goods. This is significant for monitoring and evaluation of policy measures for agri-environmental public goods as well, since most policy measures target driving forces.

Farm systems

A variety of farm systems exists within OECD countries, including intensive and extensive farming, organic farming, and various combinations of these. Some farming systems bring benefits to the environment while others cause damages. According to Cooper et al. (2009), in Europe, extensive outdoor livestock with mixed arable/pastoral systems, extensive traditional crop systems and organic systems are especially important in providing agri-environmental public goods.

For example, extensive outdoor livestock provides agricultural landscapes in some European countries.[5] Extensive systems often contribute to the conservation of the cultural and archaeological heritage (Cooper et al., 2009). The United Kingdom developed the concept of High Nature Value (HNV) farmland in the 1990s; this is low intensity farming that provides various agri-environmental public goods such as biodiversity, agricultural landscapes, water quality, flood risk reduction and carbon storage (Jones et al, 2015). Organic farming is also often associated with the provision of agri-environmental public goods (e.g. biodiversity) as it does not use chemical pesticides and inorganic fertilisers, it can manage non-cropped habitats in a non-intrusive way, and it rotates crops and adopts mixed farming (Hole et al., 2005; Cooper et al., 2009). Bengtsson et al. (2005) find that organic farm systems have 30% more species richness on average.

Farm inputs and practices

Certain farming practices and appropriate farm input management can contribute to the provision of various agri-environmental public goods. Most agri-environmental policies in the case study countries are input-based policy measures that try to improve the environment associated with agriculture. They target, for example, **tillage and irrigation practices, pesticide and nutrient application,** and **energy consumption**.

Managing soil conservation can contribute to enhancing soil quality and increasing capacities of carbon storage and stabilise the climate. Although **pesticides** can lower the risks of yield losses and are widely used in many countries, excessive use can pollute water and damage ecosystems. Thus appropriate **pesticide management** can contribute to preventing pollution and improving water quality and biodiversity.

Inputs of **nutrients**, such as **nitrogen** and **phosphorus**, are necessary to maintain and raise crop productivity. Where there is a deficit of nutrients, soil fertility declines; where there is a surplus of nutrients, there is a risk of deteriorating the water quality. In most OECD countries, there is a surplus of nutrients compared to plant requirements (OECD, 2013). The challenge is to strike a balance between increasing production and minimising negative impacts on the environment associated with nutrients (OECD, 2012; 2013).

Agriculture can play a dual role in relation to **energy**, both as a consumer and producer of energy. Farming is a direct energy consumer for crop and livestock production, and consumes energy indirectly in terms of the energy required to produce some inputs including fertilisers, pesticides and machinery. On the other hand, agriculture can produce energy and raw materials through biomass production as a feedstock to generate bioenergy, including biofuels (mainly bioethanol and biodiesel) (OECD, 2008; 2013). The key challenge for agriculture is to improve energy use efficiency by lowering energy consumption per unit of agricultural production, and seeking opportunities to increase production of biofuel feedstock in an environmentally neutral way (i.e. requires less energy to produce than the energy generated and has minimal impact in terms of environmental effects such as water and air pollution) (OECD, 2013). Efficient use of energy can contribute to better air quality and climate change.

Table 2.2 summarises some farming practices and inputs and their contribution to the provision of agri-environmental public goods. If some farming practices bring private benefits to farmers, farmers are more willing to adopt these. However, inappropriate farming practices can bring negative impacts on the environment such as water pollution and soil degradation. Some farming practices provide multiple agri-environmental public goods (ENRD, 2010; 2011).

Table 2.2. Examples of agri-environmental public goods and farming practices

Agri-environmental public goods[1]		Farming practices
Soil protection and quality	• Erosion and sediment control	• Manage soil conservation and runoff
		• Increase soil cover
Water quality	• Water quality maintenance	• Reduce agrichemical use
		• Establish vegetative buffers
		• Improve nutrient management
	• Salinisation and water table regulation	• Grow trees
		• Manage water
Water quantity/availability	• Water quantity control	• Promote efficient use of water
	• Groundwater recharge	• Keep water in paddy fields in winter
Air quality	• Odours	• Improve livestock manure management
	• Pesticides	• Improve pesticides management
Climate change - greenhouse gas emission	• Greenhouse gas emission reduction	• Capture and destroy methane from animal waste storage structures
		• Timing of fertiliser applications
		• Reduce burning
Climate change - carbon storage	• Carbon sequestration in soils	• Manage soil organic matter
		• Reduce tillage
	• Carbon sequestration in perennial plants	• Convert cropland to grassland or forest
Biodiversity	• Wildlife	• Protect breeding areas and wild food sources
		• Improve timing of cultivation
		• Increase crop species/varietal diversity
		• Reduce use of toxic chemicals
Agricultural landscape	• Land use control	• Coordinate crop species
		• Drying cultivated rice in a traditional way
Resilience to natural disasters	• Flood control	• Create diversion, wetlands, storage ponds
		• Manage irrigation systems

1. As explained in Chapter 1, these goods are not always public goods. Sometimes, they can be private goods (e.g. agricultural landscape with use value by visitors can be a private good if exclusion can be made) or when they cause harm, they can be defined as private bads or public bads (Kolstad, 2011). Careful examination on whether these goods have characteristics of non-rivalry and/or non-excludability is necessary for each case.

Source: Adapted from Food and Agriculture Organization of the United Nations (FAO) (2007), *The State of Food and Agriculture: Paying Farmers for Environmental Services*, and Ribaudo, M., et al. (2008), *The Use of Markets to Increase Private Investment in Environmental Stewardship.*

Agricultural infrastructure

Agricultural infrastructure plays a significant role in the provision of many agri-environmental public goods. For example, in the United Kingdom, historical or cultural infrastructures and management practices, such as hedges, walls, banks, ditches and other farm structures, contribute to agricultural landscapes and biodiversity (Jones et al., 2015). The appropriate management of irrigation systems is essential for water quantity control in all case study countries (Jones et al., 2015; Pannell and Roberts, 2015; Schrijver and Uetake, 2015; Shortle and Uetake, 2015; Uetake, 2015).

Farmland can contribute to the provision of agri-environmental public goods. For example, paddy fields in Japan can recharge groundwater and increase the amount of water availability (Uetake, 2015). A study estimates that about 20% of groundwater is recharged by paddy fields in Japan (Mitsubishi Research Institute, 2001).

The combination of farmland and agricultural infrastructure can also provide some agri-environmental public goods. For example, Japanese *Satoyama* landscape (mixed-community forests, arable and paddy fields, and irrigation systems) can provide a transition between different ecosystems and habitats for wildlife as well as provide risk prevention and watershed protection (OECD, 2010b).

Notes

1. Although some countries target social public goods (rural vitality, food security and animal welfare), this book focuses on agri-environmental public goods. This is because the purpose of this book is to contribute to the development of better agri-environmental policies in OECD countries, and dealing with social public goods would include a broader discussion beyond the field of agri-environmental policies. Discussing these social public goods is beyond the scope of this book.
2. This analysis focuses on agri-environmental public goods targeted by current agri-environmental policies. There may be agri-environmental public goods that OECD countries do not currently target and can be significant in the future. But, these agri-environmental public goods are out of the scope of this book.
3. Non-excludability is defined as the nature of the good is such that it is impossible to exclude anyone from consuming it. Non-rivalry is defined as the same good can be consumed by anyone without diminishing the consumption opportunities available to others.
4. Policy measures are discussed in Chapter 5.
5. This may not be the case in some countries and some areas. For example, most dairies in Australia are outdoor systems with grazing, but can be highly polluting because the nutrients can be contained, and agricultural landscapes are not targeted agri-environmental public goods.

References

Bengtsson, J., J. Ahnstrom and A. Weibull (2005), "The Effects of Organic Agriculture on Biodiversity and Abundance: A Meta-Analysis", *Journal of Applied Ecology*, Vol. 42, pp. 261-269, http://onlinelibrary.wiley.com/doi/10.1111/j.1365-2664.2005.01005.x/abstract.

Cooper, T., K. Hart and D. Baldock (2009), *The Provision of Public Goods through Agriculture in the European Union*, report prepared for DG Agriculture and Rural Development, Contract No 30-CE-023309/00-28, Institute for European Environmental Policy, London.

European Network for Rural Development (ENRD) (2011), *Thematic Working Group 3: Public Goods and Public Intervention: Synthesis Report*, ENRD, Brussels.

ENRD (2010), *Thematic Working Group 3: Public goods and Public Intervention: Final Report*, ENRD, Brussels.

Food and Agriculture Organization of the United Nations (FAO) (2007), *The State of Food and Agriculture: Paying Farmers for Environmental Services,* FAO Agriculture Series No. 38, Rome.

Gerber, A. and P.C. Wichardt (2013), "On the Private Provision of Intertemporal Public goods with Stock Effects," *Environmental Resource Economics*, Vol. 55. pp. 245-255.

Hole, D.G., A.J. Perkins, J.D. Wilson, I.H. Alexander, P.V. Grice and A.D. Evans (2005) "Does Organic Farming Benefit Biodiversity?" *Biological Conservation*, Vol. 122, pp. 113-130.

Intergovernmental Panel on Climate Change (IPCC) (2007), *Climate Change 2007: Synthesis Report*, IPCC, Geneva.

Jones, J., P. Silcock and T. Uetake (2015), "Public Goods and Externalities: Agri-environmental Policy Measures in the United Kingdom", *OECD Food, Agriculture and Fisheries Papers*, No. 83, OECD Publishing, Paris.
DOI: http://dx.doi.org/10.1787/5js08hw4drd1-en.

Kerkhof, A., E. Drissen, A.S. Uiterkamp and H. Moll (2010), "Valuation of Environmental Public Gods and Services at Different Spatial Scales: A Review", *Journal of Integrative Environmental Sciences,* Vol. 7, No. 2, pp. 125-133.

Kolstad, C. D. (2011), *Intermediate Environmental Economics: International Second Edition*, Oxford University Press, New York.

Lankoski, J., et al. (2015), "Environmental Co-benefits and Stacking in Environmental Markets", *OECD Food, Agriculture and Fisheries Papers*, No. 72, OECD Publishing, Paris.
DOI: http://dx.doi.org/10.1787/5js6g5khdvhj-en

Lewandrowski, J., M. Peter, C. Jones, R. House, M. Sperow, M. Eve and K. Paustian (2004), *Economics of Sequestering Carbon in the U.S. Agricultural Sector*, Technical Bulletin No. 909, US Department of Agriculture, Economic Research Service, Washington D.C.

Ministry of the Environment (MOE) and the United Nations University-Institute of Advanced Studies (UNU-IAS) (2010), *Satoyama Initiative*, MOE and UNU-IAS, Tokyo.

Mitsubishi Research Institute, Inc. (2001), *Evaluation of Multifunctionality associated with Agriculture and Forestry related to the Global Environment and Human Life* (in Japanese), Mitsubishi Research Institute Inc., Tokyo.

OECD (2013), *OECD Compendium of Agri-environmental Indicators*, OECD Publishing, Paris. DOI: http://dx.doi.org/10.1787/9789264186217-en.

OECD (2012), *Water Quality and Agriculture: Meeting the Policy Challenge*, OECD Studies on Water, OECD Publishing, Paris.
DOI: http://dx.doi.org/10.1787/9789264168060-en.

OECD (2010a), *Sustainable Management of Water Resources in Agriculture*, OECD Studies on Water, OECD Publishing, Paris.
DOI: http://dx.doi.org/10.1787/9789264083578-en.

OECD (2010b), *OECD Environmental Performance Reviews: Japan 2010*, OECD Publishing, Paris.
DOI: http://dx.doi.org/10.1787/9789264087873-en.

OECD (2010c), *Guidelines for Cost-effective Agri-environmental Policy Measures*, OECD Publishing, Paris.
DOI: http://dx.doi.org/10.1787/9789264086845-en.

OECD (2008), *Environmental Performance of Agriculture in OECD Countries Since 1990*, OECD Publishing, Paris.
DOI: http://dx.doi.org/10.1787/9789264040854-en.

OECD (2005), *Multifunctionality in Agriculture: What Role for Private Initiatives?*, OECD Publishing, Paris.
DOI: http://dx.doi.org/10.1787/9789264014473-en.

Pannell, D. and A. Roberts (2015), "Public goods and externalities: agri-environmental policy measures in Australia", *OECD Food, Agriculture and Fisheries Papers*, No. 80, OECD Publishing, Paris.
DOI: http://dx.doi.org/10.1787/5js08hx1btlw-en.

Ribaudo, M., L. Hansen, D. Hellerstein and C. Greene (2008), *The Use of Markets to Increase Private Investment in Environmental Stewardship*, United States Department of Agriculture, Economic Research Service, Economic Research Report Number 64, Washington D.C.

Schrijver, R. and T. Uetake (2015), "Public goods and externalities: agri-environmental policy measures in the Netherlands", *OECD Food, Agriculture and Fisheries Papers*, No. 82, OECD Publishing, Paris.
DOI: http://dx.doi.org/10.1787/5js08hwpr1q8-en.

Shortle, J. and T. Uetake (2015), "Public Goods and Externalities: Agri-environmental Policy Measures in the the United States", *OECD Food, Agriculture and Fisheries Papers*, No. 84, OECD Publishing, Paris.
DOI: http://dx.doi.org/10.1787/5js08hwhg8mw-en.

Trumper, K., M. Bertzky, B. Dickson, G. van der Heijden, M. Jenkins and P. Manning (2009), *The Natural Fix? The Role of Ecosystems in Climate Mitigation*, A UNEP rapid response assessment, United Nations Environment Programme, UNEP-WCMC, Cambridge, UK.

Uetake, T. (2015), "Public goods and externalities: agri-environmental policy measures in Japan", *OECD Food, Agriculture and Fisheries Papers*, No. 81, OECD Publishing, Paris.
DOI: http://dx.doi.org/10.1787/5js08hwsjj26-en.

Vojtech, V. (2010), “Policy Measures Addressing Agri-environmental Issues”, *OECD Food, Agriculture and Fisheries Papers*, No. 24, OECD Publishing, Paris.
DOI: http://dx.doi.org/10.1787/5kmjrzg08vvb-en.

Chapter 3

Market failure associated with agri-environmental public goods

This chapter analyses how countries estimate demand and supply of agri-environmental public goods, and how they examine whether market failures associated with the agri-environmental public goods exist. It discusses the importance of identifying the extent farmers can voluntarily provide agri-environmental public goods without government intervention.

The market for agri-environmental public goods

Although agriculture can provide agri-environmental public goods, markets for these goods are, generally speaking, under-developed and this makes it difficult for famers to produce adequate amount public goods (OECD, 1992, 1999, 2013a; Ribaudo et al., 2008). Non-excludability (the nature of the good is such that it is impossible to exclude anyone from consuming it), non-rivalry (the same good can be consumed by anyone without diminishing the consumption opportunities available to others) and other factors such as asymmetric information and information failure reduce the effectiveness of markets (Bergstrom and Randall, 2010). Under imperfect markets, the value of agri-environmental public goods is often not reflected in agricultural commodity and land prices. As such prices do not properly convey the value of agri-environmental public goods, including its future value, this may result in the under or over-supply of agri-environmental public goods (Hellerstein et al., 2002).

Nevertheless, the provision of agri-environmental public goods does not necessarily mean governments should intervene. Two issues should be examined. First, although in theory it is difficult to produce an adequate amount of agri-environmental public goods due to non-excludability and non-rivalry, farmers can provide the right amount incidentally. Some farming practices bring both on- and off-farm benefits. If farmers fully take into consideration private benefits, there is a possibility that farmers will produce an adequate amount of agri-environmental public goods without government intervention. Estimating both the demand and supply of agri-environmental public goods is necessary (Hodge and Reader, 2007). To justify government intervention, evidence of market failure is necessary.

Second, government intervention involves additional costs, and may worsen social welfare as compared to what existed prior to the intervention. Benefits from the intervention must outweigh the costs. The cost of not intervening, particularly in the long run, must also be taken into account in the cost-benefits analysis.

It is difficult to estimate the scale of demand and supply of agri-environmental public goods because of the absence of markets. As a result, examining whether market failure associated with agri-environmental public goods exists or not is challenging. In reality, instead of data which directly estimates the demand and supply of agri-environmental public goods, some proxies are often used.

This chapter illustrates recent efforts to examine whether market failure associated with agri-environmental public goods exists or not in the OECD case study countries. First, the demand for agri-environmental public goods is examined for the identified agri-environmental public goods in Chapter 2. Second, the supply side of agri-environmental public goods is reviewed. Finally, market failures are examined. Since estimating demand for public goods is especially difficult, more focus has been placed on the supply side, i.e. agri-environmental indicators. The book reveals that, in most cases, examination of the two issues, i.e. whether supply of agri-environmental public goods by farmers meets demand and whether benefits from government intervention outweigh the costs, is lacking.

Assessing the demand for agri-environmental public goods

Assessing the scale of demand for agri-environmental public goods is a challenge because of the characteristics of public goods, i.e. non-rivalry and non-excludability. There are no actual markets for these goods where consumers can express their demand for public goods (Cooper et al., 2009). There are mainly two approaches for estimating the demand: using proxy indicators (e.g. visitor numbers to natural resource areas) and monetary valuation studies (Hall et al., 2004; Cooper et al., 2009; McVittie et al., 2009; Hübner and Kantelhardt, 2010; Hart et al., 2011). However, due to the difficulties of estimating the demand of agri-environmental public goods, both approaches have limitations and their application to policy design is limited in the OECD case study countries.

Proxy indicators

One approach for estimating the demand for agri-environmental public goods is to look at representative indicators or expressions of mass behaviour (Hall et al., 2004; Cooper et al., 2009; McVittie et al., 2009; Hübner and Kantelhardt, 2010; Hart et al., 2011). Although these numbers do not precisely calculate the demand for agri-environmental public goods, they can offer an overall picture on trends or perceptions among people.

Various proxies are used in the OECD case study countries examined (Table 3.1 summarises the selected examples of proxy indicators). Demand for agri-environmental public goods can be expressed through, for example, public-opinion polls, membership in environmental NGOs, the purchase of conservation easements by land trusts, and the number of visitors to protected areas (Piperno and Santagata, 1992; Ribaudo et al., 2008; Cooper et al., 2009; Hübner and Kantelhardt, 2010; Hart et al., 2011). There are several public-opinion polls which survey environmental concerns and the expected role of agriculture. Typically, there are multiple choices so that it is possible to understand the public's priorities.

Another proxy indicator is membership in various natural conservation movements and the purchased areas for conservation. Increasing numbers of land trusts and purchased areas indicate there is demand for agri-environmental public goods. Individuals can participate in environmental NGOs and land trusts that contribute to the conservation of natural resources associated with agriculture (Hein et al., 2006; Sundberg, 2006). There are many land trusts in OECD countries. For example, the National Trust in the United Kingdom is the world's largest conservation society, having 3.9 million members, 67 000 volunteers and managing over 250 000 hectares of land in 2011/12 (Jones et al., 2015). In the United States, there are about 1 700 land trusts, protecting open space and habitat covering over 47 million acres of land as of 2010, an increase from 37 million acres in 2005, and 24 million acres in 2000 (Land Trust Alliance, 2010).

Numbers of visitors to protected areas such as national parks also provide an indication of the demand for agri-environmental public goods to some extent (Hübner and Kantelhardt, 2010). For example, national parks in England attracted 95 million visitors who spent GBP 4 billion in 2011. Some of these visitors visited the parks to enjoy agricultural landscapes and biodiversity, thus, the number of visitors and the amount of money spent by them can indirectly show the demand of agri-environmental public goods (Jones et al., 2015).

If we can understand the trends of these proxy indicators, it may be possible to find how public perceptions of agri-environmental public goods has changed over the years, although they do not necessarily show to what extent the public demands each agri-environmental public good. Some categories of proxy indicators are too general (for example, the EC public opinion polls (EC, 2009; 2011) did not distinguish greenhouse gas emissions and carbon storage). Even within the same category of an agri-environmental public good, preferences are diverse. For example, regarding agricultural landscapes, Howley et al. (2012) revealed that the Irish prefer more traditional extensive farming landscapes over modern intensive farming landscapes. Environmental preferences are different depending on social and demographic characteristics of population, such as age, income, place of residence and the presence of children (Howley et al., 2012; Howley et al., 2014). Demand may vary depending on different scales (local, national, or global), but most proxy indicators do not reflect these differences. Furthermore, proxy indicators are not always statistically robust (Hall et al., 2004), and there are possibilities that other factors affect the proxies. For example, membership in conservation groups and visits to national parks may represent non-agri-environmental issues such as population density issues, and may not reflect the demand of agri-environmental public goods that much. Thus, careful interpretation of the proxy indicators is necessary.

What kind of proxy indicators should be used is still under discussion, and no consensus has been established. It is important to clarify the merits and limitations of various proxy indicators. More studies on appropriate proxy indicators may be able to contribute to a better understanding of the demand for agri-environmental public goods.

Table 3.1. Selected examples of proxy indicators for agri-environmental public goods

Indicators	Country	Agri-environmental public goods[1]	Note	Data
Public-opinion polls	Japan	Biodiversity and agricultural landscape	Percentage of respondents expecting the role of agriculture and rural areas that can preserve biodiversity and provide landscapes	48.9% (2008)[a]
		Water quantity/availability and resilience to natural disasters	Percentage of respondents expecting the role of agriculture and rural areas that preserve water resources and prevent natural disasters such as landslide and flood	29.6% (2008)[a]
	Netherlands	Agricultural landscapes	Percentage of respondents concerned about depletion of natural resources	49% (2011)[b]
		Water quality	Percentage of respondents concerned about water pollution	40% (2011)[b]
		Climate change	Percentage of respondents concerned about climate change	37% (2011)[b]
		Air quality	Percentage of respondents concerned about air pollution	34% (2011)[b]
		Biodiversity	Percentage of respondents concerned about loss of biodiversity	29% (2011)[b]
	United Kingdom	Climate change	Percentage of respondents concerned about climate change	53%(2009)[c]
		Air quality	Percentage of respondents concerned about air pollution	42%(2009)[c]
		Water quality	Percentage of respondents concerned about water pollution	35%(2009)[c]
		Agricultural landscapes	Percentage of respondents concerned about depletion of natural resources	27%(2009)[c]
		Biodiversity	Percentage of respondents concerned about loss of biodiversity	20%(2009)[c]
Membership in nature conservation movement	United Kingdom	Biodiversity and agricultural landscape	Increasing membership in nature conservation movement can be proxy of increasing demand for agricultural landscape and biodiversity	5 million (2006/07) to 6 million (2011/12)[d]
Purchase of conservation easements by land trusts	United States	Biodiversity, habitats, wetlands	Purchased areas by land trust for protecting open space and habitat.	24 million acres(2000) to 47 million acres of land (2010)[e]
Visitor numbers to protected areas	England	Agricultural landscape	Visitor numbers of national parks can provide an indication of the scale of public demand for landscapes (many of which are agricultural).	95 million visitors (2011)[d]

1. As explained in Chapter 1, these goods are not always public goods. Sometimes, they can be private goods (e.g. agricultural landscape with use value by visitors can be a private good if exclusion can be made) or when they cause harm, they can be defined as private bads or public bads (Kolstad, 2011). Careful examination on whether these goods have characteristics of non-rivalry and/or non-excludability is necessary for each case.

Sources:

a. CAO (2008), *Public Opinion Poll regarding the Role of Food, Agriculture and Rural areas.* http://www8.cao.go.jp/survey/h20/h20-shokuryou/index.html.

b. European Commission (2011), *Attitudes of European Citizens towards the Environment*, Special Eurobarometer 365, European Commission, Brussels.

c. European Commission (2009), *The Europeans in 2009.*

d. Jones et al. (2015), *Public Goods and Externalities: Agri-environmental Policy Measures in the United Kingdom*,.

e. Land Trust Alliance (2010), *2010 National Land Trust Census Report: A look at Voluntary Land Conservation in America.*

Monetary valuation

The other approach to estimating demand for agri-environmental public goods is to apply monetary valuation methodologies to reveal social preferences (Box 3.1 briefly explains main monetary valuation methodologies). Some economic techniques can estimate the demand curve of public goods (Turner et al., 1993; Kolstad, 2011).

There are several studies which examine the demand for agri-environmental public goods by using monetary valuations.[1] For example, in the United Kingdom, a series of studies have estimated the average willingness to pay (WTP) values per household for some agri-environmental public goods, such as agricultural landscapes and biodiversity. These WTP values are of some interest to policy makers and policy designers, but they are not used to developing payment rates for agri-environmental policies. This is because the Common Agricultural Policy (CAP) requires such rates to be based on income foregone and additional costs (Council Regulation (EC) No 1698/2005, Article 39). Under WTO green box rules, payments under environmental programmes are limited to the extra costs or loss of income involved in complying with a government programme (Article 6 and Annex 2 of the agreement on agriculture).[2] In the Netherlands, few studies have focused on demand estimates for agri-environmental public goods (Pannell and Roberts, 2015).

Some demand for agri-environmental public goods can be estimated based on econometric analysis on actual market behaviour. For example, Artell (2013) estimated the water quality value in Finland by using the travel cost and hedonic price methods.

There are some new projects that use monetary valuation for better policies as well. For example, The BalticSTERN Secretariat, established in 2009, co-ordinates an international research network and produces ecological-socioeconomic analysis of cost-effective measures for ensuring the provision of ecosystem services in the Baltic Sea. A series of studies has been undertaken, including Ahtiainen et al. (2012) that uses state-of-the-art marine modelling with environmental valuation techniques to provide a value for improving the state of the Baltic Sea to good ecological status by the year 2050. The study involved over 10 000 respondents from all of the littoral countries of the Baltic Sea and estimated the benefits of reducing eutrophication in the Baltic Sea.

Monetary valuations, however, have problems. One must carefully interpret these numbers, especially values which provide aggregate numbers, since good policy measures provide incentives to target marginal changes and behaviours. The distinction of these two values is not always made in the literature (Sakuyama 2005; Goulder and Kennedy, 2011). It is also known that monetary values change depending on the adopted methodologies, questions and procedures as well as socio-economic characteristics of individuals (Diamond and Hausman, 1994; Moran et al., 2007; Arriaza et al., 2008; Cooper et al., 2009; Howley et al., 2012). The spatial scale of agri-environmental public goods also affects valuation (Hein et al., 2006). Various numbers can be drawn for a same agri-environmental public good. Direct comparison of these numbers among countries and regions is not possible either, although this can be possible for proxy indicators. As a result, there is no comprehensive monetary assessment of the costs and benefits of agri-environmental public goods (OECD, 2013b). Some researchers disagree with using monetary valuation in policy design (e.g. Diamond and Hausman, 1994), while others argue these limitations can be overcome by careful research design (e.g. Arrow et al., 1993; Kling et al., 2012).

There is also the problem of a biased focus. Much focus is placed on agri-environmental public goods that are already provided, but less on future and upcoming priorities (OECD, 1992). Often, studies on monetary valuation rely on a certain baseline and take current levels of provision of agri-environmental public goods for granted. However, the baseline is not set in many cases. Finding appropriate counterfactual data is one of the main challenges for conducting environmental valuation (Sakuyama, 2005; RISE, 2009; Hübner and Kantelhardt, 2010; OECD, 2012).

Box 3.1. Monetary valuation of agri-environmental public goods

There are two broad methodological strategies for monetary valuation methods:[1] revealed preference methods and stated preference methods. Revealed preference methods are the valuation of non-market impacts by observing actual behaviour and, in particular, purchases made in actual markets (OECD, 2006). Stated preference methods utilise questionnaires which either directly ask respondents for their willingness to pay (WTP) or willingness to accept (WTA), or offer them choices between "bundles" of attributes (inferences are drawn from the options selected) WTP (WTA) (OECD, 2006).

There are several approaches with each of these categories. Table 3.2 summarises four main methods for estimating monetary values of environmental services. Sometimes, these methods are combined (e.g. Cameron, 1992, Kling, 1997). For instance, Fleischer and Tsur (2000) estimated the demand of agricultural landscape in Israel by using CVM and travel cost method. Covering these methodologies in detail is beyond the scope of this book. For more description and discussions on monetary valuation, please refer to *Cost-benefit Analysis and the Environment: Recent Developments* (OECD, 2006), which explains all kinds of monetary valuation methodologies in detail.

Table 3.2. Main monetary valuation methods where a demand curve is available

Stated preference methods		Revealed preference methods	
Can be used for both use and non-use values		Can be only used for use values	
Contingent valuation (CVM)	Choice modelling (Conjoint analysis)	Travel cost method	Hedonic price method
Estimates the WTP (WTA) by using a questionnaire and asking respondents directly how much money they are willing to pay (willing to accept).	Inferring the WTP (WTA) by using a questioner which offers respondents choices between bundles of attributes.	Estimates the value of the use of non-market goods, particularly geographical areas and locations used for recreational purposes by observing the costs of travelling.	Estimates the value of the use of non-market goods by observing behaviour in the market for a related good.
E.g. estimating the WTP for biodiversity conservation by asking how much money local people are willing to pay.	E.g. estimating the WTP for biodiversity conservation by showing several scenarios that have different levels of attribute such as outcomes and costs	E.g. estimating the value of use-value of agricultural landscape by observing the data on costs of travelling.	E.g. estimating the impact of water quality on residential property by looking at property values with different water quality.

WTP– Willingness to Pay, WTA– Willingness to Accept.

Source: Adapted from Turner, R.K., D. Pearce and I. Bateman (1993), *Environmental Economics: An Elementary Introduction*, OECD (2006), *Cost-Benefit Analysis and the Environment: Recent Developments*, and Bateman, I.J. et al. (2011), "Economic Analysis for Ecosystem Service Assessments".

When estimating the demand, the scale of agri-environmental public goods is important. Some agri-environmental public goods are local public goods (e.g. agricultural landscape, resilience to natural disasters), while others are regional or global (e.g. climate change, water quality) (Madureira et al., 2013). With appropriate scale of estimation, the demand for an agri-environmental public good can be estimated.

1. There are monetary valuation methods where a demand curve is not available. These include dose-response method, replacement costs and avoidance costs. Although they are practically informative for policy makers in some cases, this book does not cover them because they cannot measure the demand of agri-environmental public goods directly.

Policy objectives and targets

Because of the limitations of proxy indicators and monetary valuation, several previous studies (e.g. OECD, 1992; Ribaudo et al., 2008; Hart et al., 2011) state that policy objectives and targets can be used as a proxy to identify social demand and the socially optimal level of provision of agri-environmental public goods, since these are determined through the political decision-making process and reflect collective demand. OECD (1992) argues that the political process can give rise to a demand for public goods, and this can overcome one of the most difficult issues, i.e. knowledge gaps of the public goods market. Many countries develop agri-environmental programmes and set agri-environmental policy objectives and targets, which implicitly reflecting public demands (Ribaudo et al., 2008). For example, in EU countries, the relevant objectives and targets are set at both the EU and national levels. They comprise both explicit and implicit targets, and some are legally binding and others not. According to Hart et al. (2011), explicit EU targets have been set predominantly in relation to biodiversity, water quality, greenhouse gas emissions, and air quality; in many cases they have specific and quantified goals, and in certain cases they need to meet a specified timeframe. Proxy indicators such as public opinion polls and monetary valuation can help policy makers to identify policy objectives and develop policy measures for agri-environmental public goods.

These policy objectives and targets, however, do not necessarily reflect demand of the general public. Several interest groups influence policy design through lobbies. They do not necessarily have common interests. Policy makers, thus, need to weigh the significance of each good and take into consideration future generations (OECD, 1992).

Studies on the demand for agri-environmental public goods are still in progress and its application to agri-environmental policy design is limited. More studies in this field and discussion on how to use the estimates in agri-environmental policy design are necessary.

Assessing the supply of agri-environmental public goods

In order to identify whether incidental provision of agri-environmental public goods meet demand or not requires analysis on the supply side. Regarding the supply side of agri-environmental public goods, one way to examine the scale of supply is to use agri-environmental indicators (Cooper et al., 2009; Hart et al., 2011).

Notably, OECD agri-environmental indicators (OECD, 2013b) can be used to examine the status of agri-environmental public goods in a comparative way. But, since some agri-environmental public goods are local public goods, aggregated national-level indicators such as OECD agri-environmental indicators may not be appropriate to estimate the supply (Saunders et al., 2009).

In addition to the OECD agri-environmental indicators, various indicators are also used but differ depending on the country and their priorities and perceptions of agri-environmental public goods. Table 3.3 summarises the indicators which are used to estimate the supply of agri-environmental public goods in the case study countries. These indicators can be grouped by either pressure indicators (measuring driving forces) or condition indicators (measuring agri-environmental public goods) (Figure 2.1).

Pressure indicators include indicators for nutrients (nitrogen and phosphorus balance), pesticides, energy, farmland, and irrigation systems. Condition indicators include soil erosion, agricultural freshwater withdrawals, GHG emissions and farmland birds. Since some agri-environmental public goods are local or global, local-level and global-level data are necessary to estimate supply. For example, regarding resilience to natural disasters, the actual number of flood events or area of forest burned is necessary for each provided scale.

Table 3.3 shows the application of some of indicators for understanding supply trends in the United Kingdom. Overall, there is a mixed picture, with some agri-environmental public goods increasing and others decreasing.

However, using these indicators to assess the current level of provision of agri-environmental public goods needs caution. First, many provide information at a national scale only, as is the case for the United Kingdom (Table 3.4). Trends may differ considerably at farm, local or global levels. Second, many indicators are not sensitive enough to capture changes in the environmental media. For example, Saunders et al. (2009) tried to assess the performance of individual kiwifruit orchards in New Zealand by using OECD agri-environmental indicators, but these were not able to examine field-level variations across orchards. How driving forces affect agri-environmental public goods is difficult to measure. Third, for many indicators, data have not been collected over time. Most data only provide a snap-shot of the current level of provision. Fourth, within biological and hydrological systems, there is often a considerable time lag between the causative farm management practices and the observed environmental impact. Lastly, most data does not consider quality. For instance, each parcel of farmland differs in environmental quality. Aggregated data does not consider the heterogeneity of qualities of environmental conditions (Cooper et al., 2009; OECD, 2013b). For a more detailed picture, more carefully designed investment in data is required at regular intervals.

Table 3.3. Examples of indicators used for estimating the supply of agri-environmental public goods

Agri-environmental public goods[1]	Indicators[2]	
	Pressure indicators (driving forces)	**Condition indicators (agri-environmental public goods)**
Soil protection and quality	• *Gross nitrogen balance* • *Gross phosphorus balance* • *Agricultural land affected by water and wind erosion*	• Soil organic matter
Water quality	• *Gross nitrogen balance* • *Gross phosphorus balance* • *Total sales of agricultural pesticides*	• *Nitrate, phosphorus and pesticide pollution derived from agriculture in surface water, groundwater and marine waters*
Water quantity/ availability	• *Irrigated land area* • *Irrigation water application rate*	• *Total agricultural water withdrawals* • *Agricultural share of total freshwater withdrawals* • Water retaining capacity (paddy fields)
Air quality	• *Total sales of agricultural pesticides* • Areas of land burned • Shares of livestock farms with adequate manure treatment facilities	• *Agricultural ammonia emissions* • Number of complaints related to offensive livestock odours • Number of affected people in their living environment related to offensive livestock odours • Emission trends of air pollutants
Climate change – greenhouse gas emissions	• *Direct on-farm energy consumption* • *Methyl bromide use*	• *Total agricultural GHG emissions* • *Methane emissions from agriculture* • *Nitrous oxide emissions from agriculture*
Climate change – carbon storage	• Conversion of farmland to urban use	• Arable and horticultural soil carbon storage
Biodiversity	• *Agricultural land cover types* • *Total sales of agricultural pesticides* • Conversion of farmland to urban use • Conversion of grassland to arable land • Area of wetlands and other habitats converted to agricultural uses • Destruction of natural infrastructure	• *Population of farmland birds* • Farmland butterflies • Share of freshwater fish species listed on the national Red List
Agricultural landscapes	• *Agricultural land use area* • Conversion of farmland to urban use • Abandoned farmland	• Agricultural landscape change
Resilience to natural disasters	• *Agricultural land use area* • Conversion of farmland to urban use • Irrigation systems exceeding their lifespans	• Numbers of flood events • Area of forest burned

1. As explained in Chapter 1, these goods are not always public goods. Sometimes, they can be private goods (e.g. agricultural landscape with use value by visitors can be a private good if exclusion can be made) or when they cause harm, they can be defined as private bads or public bads (Kolstad, 2011). Careful examination on whether these goods have characteristics of non-rivalry and/or non-excludability is necessary for each case.

2. Indicators are used in some studied OECD countries. They do not reflect OECD views nor OECD member countries' views.

3. *Italic:* OECD agri-environmental indicators; Non-italic: other indicators.

Table 3.4. Trends of agri-environmental public goods in the United Kingdom

Agri-environmental public goods[1]	Trends	Related indicators		Sources
Soil quality and protection	+/-	• Gross nitrogen balance • Gross phosphorus balance • Farmland at moderate or high risk of soil erosion • *Soil organic matter*	• -30% (1990-2009) • -54% (1990-2009) • 6% (1999) to 17% (2002) • *-0.5% in England and Wales (1979/81-1995)*	• OECD(2013b) • OECD(2013b) • OECD (2013b) • EA (2004) • UKNEA (2011)
Water quality	↗	• Gross nitrogen balance • Gross phosphorus balance • Total sales of agricultural pesticides • Share of agriculture in total emissions of phosphorous in surface water	• -30% (1990-2009) • -54% (1990-2009) • -56% (1990-2010) • 29% (2000) to 19.5%(2009)	• OECD(2013b) • OECD(2013b) • OECD(2013b) • UKNEA (2011) • OECD(2013b)
Water quantity /availability	+/-	• *Total agricultural water withdrawals* • *Agricultural share of total freshwater withdrawals*	• *-4% (from 1990/92 to 2006/8)* • *12% (1990/2) to 15% (2006/8)*	• OECD (2013b) • OECD (2013b) • UKNEA (2011)
Air quality	↗	• *Total ammonia emissions from agriculture*	• *-24% (from 1990 to 2011)*	• OECD(2013b) • Defra et al. 2013) • UKNEA (2011)
Climate change – greenhouse gas emissions	↗	• *Total GHG emissions from agriculture* • *Methane emissions from agriculture* • *Nitrous oxide emissions from agriculture* • Direct on-farm energy consumption	• *-20%(from 1990 to 2010)* • *-20% (from 1990 to 2010)* • *-20% (from 1990 to 2010)* • -23% (from 1990 to 2010)	• OECD(2013b) • OECD(2013b) • OECD(2013b) • UKNEA (2011) • OECD(2013b)
Climate change – carbon storage	~	• *Arable and horticultural soil carbon storage*	• *Slight decline in England over 1978-2007*	• Defra (2013)
Biodiversity	↘	• *Farmland birds* • *Farmland butterflies*	• *-36% (1990-2011) and -50% (1970-2011)* • *-25% (1970-2011)*	• OECD(2013b) • Defra et al. (2013) • RSPB (2013)
Agricultural landscapes	+/-	• Farmland area • *Agricultural landscape change*	• -6% (1990-2012) • *Positive change in 64% of National Character Areas in England over 1999-2004*	• OECD (2013b) • Defra et al. (2013) • Defra (2012) • UKNEA (2011)
Resilience to natural disasters	~	• Farmland area	• -6% (1990-2012)	• OECD(2013b)/ • Defra et al. (2013) • UKNEA (2011)

Note:  Decreasing  Increasing).  Both increasing and decreasing data  No or insufficient data

1. As explained in Chapter 1, these goods are not always public goods. Sometimes, they can be private goods (e.g. agricultural landscape with use value by visitors can be a private good if exclusion can be made) or when they cause harm, they can be defined as private bads or public bads (Kolstad, 2011). Careful examination on whether these goods have characteristics of non-rivalry and/or non-excludability is necessary for each case.
2. *Italic: Condition indicators (agri-environmental public goods)*; Non-italic: Pressure indicators (driving forces).

Source: Adapted from Jones et al. (2015), *Public Goods and Externalities: Agri-environmental Policy Measures in the United Kingdom*.

Table 3.4. Trends of agri-environmental public goods in the United Kingdom (cont.)

Data from:

Defra (2013), *England Natural Environment Indicators*, Defra, London.
Defra (2012), *Observatory Monitoring Framework: Environmental impact: Landscape Indicator DF3: Landscape change*, Defra, London.
DEFRA/DARD/SG/WAG (2013), *Agriculture in the United Kingdom 2012*, Defra, Department of Agriculture and Rural Development (Northern Ireland), The Scottish Government, Rural and Environment Research and Analysis Directorate, Welsh Assembly Government, The Department for Rural Affairs and Heritage.
Environment Agency (EA) (2004), *The State of Soils in England and Wales*, Environment Agency, Bristol.
OECD (2013b), *OECD Compendium of Agri-environmental Indicators*, OECD Publishing, Paris. doi: 10.1787/9789264186217-en.
RSPB (2013), *RSPB Facts and Figures*, RSPB, Bedfordshire.
UK National Ecosystem Assessment (2011), *The UK National Ecosystem Assessment: Synthesis of the Key Findings*. UNEP-WCMC, Cambridge.

When should government intervene?

Estimating the scale of demand and supply of agri-environmental public goods is, as mentioned above, difficult. In addition, whether the supply meets demand or not must be examined for each agri-environmental public good at the appropriate scale.[3] Some agri-environmental public goods are global so that national or trans-boundary data would be necessary to examine this point. Others are local public goods, thus, local level or farm level data is needed to investigate the extent of market failure. Therefore, it is difficult to conclude that there is a situation of undersupply or overprovision of agri-environmental public goods in the five case study countries.

This examination process, however, is important, since the provision of agri-environmental public goods does not necessarily mean governments should always intervene. Although in theory it is difficult to produce an adequate amount of agri-environmental public goods because of the non-excludable and non-rival characteristics of public goods, farmers can provide the right amount incidentally. Indeed, there is a case where farmers can produce some agri-environmental public goods voluntarily. For instance, adoption of zero tillage and minimum tillage practices can contribute to reduced soil erosion, the prevention of dust storms, better air quality, and increased soil carbon storage. This is widely adopted by some farmers, for example in Australia and the United States, but the main reasons for farmers adopting zero and reduced tillage are related to its economic advantages such as the relative effectiveness of pre-emergent herbicides and reduced costs for fuel and labour (D'Emden et al., 2008; Ebel, 2012; Pannell and Roberts, 2015; Shortle and Uetake, 2015). If farmers take private benefits associated with public goods provision, there is a possibility that farmers provide more agri-environmental public goods without government support and meet demand voluntarily. If government intervenes even in this case, there is a risk of too much government intervention.

This examination process also clarifies the priority areas of policy intervention, if any (OECD, 1994). Although it is difficult to estimate accurate quantities for demand and supply, the process may be able to identify rough trends. It is easy to state that government intervention is necessary for public goods, but priorities and the extent of intervention can vary depending on the market failure of each agri-environmental public good. By examining the demand and supply of agri-environmental public goods, it can be clearer for which agri-environmental public goods the largest gap of demand and supply exists. This helps governments decide on which agri-environmental public goods to focus. As noted above, such examinations are not widespread in the OECD case study countries covered in this book.

In addition, even if there is undersupply of agri-environmental public goods, government intervention involves additional costs. Therefore, the expected benefits of a policy need to outweigh its expected costs. If a policy brings larger benefits than costs, it can improve social welfare as compared to before the intervention (Pagiola et al., 2004; OECD, 2006; 2010). The cost of not intervening must also be taken into consideration in the analysis. For example, Stern (2006) argues that the costs of stabilising the climate are significant, but the costs of inaction can be more significant. Government intervention can be justified if cases of non-government intervention bring larger costs than those of government intervention (Weimer and Vining, 2010; Keech et al., 2012). Whether the government intervention brings larger benefits than costs is an empirical question and has to be examined for each case.

Some countries, such as Australia and the United States, state they try to undertake cost-benefit analysis before government intervention. For example, the Australian *Best Practice Regulation Handbook* (Australian Government, 2013) states that the Australian Government uses cost–benefit analysis to assess regulatory proposals for encouraging better decision-making, including taking all effects including non-direct effects into account. In practice the conduct of such analysis is limited, with analyses relying on limited existing data and resources, and not necessarily drawing robust conclusions. The United Kingdom has been trying to better integrate impacts on the natural environment in decision-making, but the work is at an early stage (Defra, 2007; 2010). The application of cost-benefit analysis is limited in Japan and the Netherlands.

Government intervenes to resolve market failures in order to provide an adequate amount of agri-environmental public goods. Sometimes, however, government intervention makes situations worse. Government failure is a situation where government intervention creates inefficiency. For example, Olmstead (2010) examined water quality protection in the United States by examining the existing literature. She argued that the Clean Water Act (CWA) had brought net benefits up to the late 1980s, but that afterwards the incremental costs exceeded the incremental benefits. Appropriate targeting of both point source and non-point source pollution and policy choices are key factors that must be taken into account to overcome government failure in this area, and innovative approaches, such as performance-based instruments and water quality trading, would offer the possibility of improving the effectiveness and efficiency of water quality programmes in the United Sates (Shortle and Uetake, 2015). Government inaction can also result in Pareto inferior outcomes and can be regarded as passive government failure (Weimer and Vining, 2010; Keech et al., 2012).

Policy makers take into consideration various criteria including environmental effectiveness and cost-effectiveness of policy measures, administration costs and constraints and social factors such as equity and income distribution (OECD, 2006; 2010). Some agri-environmental policies also place an emphasis on community engagement and capacity building. The fundamental challenge for policy makers is to develop policy measures for agri-environmental public goods that can achieve environmental goals with the least overall costs, including farmers' compliance costs and policy related transaction costs, taking into account equity consideration and other social factors (OECD, 2010).

Box 3.2. Paying for ecosystem services: The United Kingdom's Upstream Thinking Project

In the rural areas of south-west England, intensive livestock and dairy farms can be a major source of diffuse water pollution in the form of sediment, nutrients and faecal organisms. The "Upstream Thinking Project" is a new approach to improving raw water resources with the aim of improving raw water quality and managing the quantity of water at source through improved land management.

Traditionally, water companies rely on costly energy and chemicals to treat poor quality raw water. Improving land management, however, can reduce surface run-off and water pollution, and thus the amount of resources needed to treat water to safe drinking standards. In collaboration with the Westcountry Rivers Trust (WRT), an environmental non-government organisation, the South West Water initiated a programme to promote better land management by farmers to inform and assist them in the protection of catchments as part of an integrated approach to good land management. As beneficiary and buyer of ecosystem services, the South West Water recognised the economic, ecological and regulatory benefit of improved raw water quality. They provide tailored one-to-one advice and help farmers to develop farm plans that focus on both the environment and the objectives of the farm business. Farmers' actions are supported by financial assistance (Payment for Ecosystem Services). Payments are based on action through investment in improved farm infrastructure and agricultural practice rather than ecosystem service outputs. This project can improve both the economic and environmental sustainability of water in South West England, as well as provide ecosystem services such as biodiversity, carbon sequestration and the reduction of the risk of flooding.

Source: OECD (2013a), *Providing Agri-environmental Public Goods through Collective Action*.

Finally, some agri-environmental public goods can be provided with the assistance of the private sector (OECD, 2005; 2013a). For example, there is growing interest in the emergence of the privately funded Payment for Ecosystem Service (PES) schemes in the United Kingdom. Several pilot schemes are operating, mainly by water companies such as the Upstream Thinking Project run by South West Water (OECD, 2013a) (Box 3.2). Although the role of the private sector in providing agri-environmental public goods is beyond the scope of this book, it is an important area that should be examined further. It may be able to show an alternative approach to dealing with market failures associated with agri-environmental public goods.

Notes

1. Environmental Valuation Reference Inventory (EVRI) provides various valuation study results. Environment Canada has developed the EVRI in collaboration with a number of international experts and organisations including Department for Environment, Food & Rural Affairs (United Kingdom), Department of Sustainability, Environment, Water, Population and Communities (Australia), Environmental Protection Agency (United States), Ministère de l'Écologie, du Développement durable et de l'Énergie (France) and Ministry for the Environment (New Zealand).
2. Discussion on how to use WTP values in agri-environmental policy designs needs careful and broad research, including discussions on trade policies. This is beyond the scope of this book.
3. Some countries try to examine landscape-level management for agri-environmental public goods beyond farm-level management. For example, the EU-funded CLAIM project tries to support an effective CAP policy design to improve landscape-level management.

References

Ahtiainen, H. et al. (2012), "Benefits of Meeting the Baltic Sea Nutrient Reduction Targets – Combining Ecological Modelling and Contingent Valuation in the Nine Littoral States", *MTT Discussion Papers 1*, MTT Agrifood Research Finland, Jokioinen.

Artell, J. (2013), *Recreation Value and Quality of Finnish Surface Waters: Revealed Preferences, Individual Perceptions and Spatial Issues*, MIT Science, No.23, MIT Agrifood Research Finland.

Arriaza, M. et al. (2008), "Demand for Non-commodity Outputs from Mountain Olive Groves", *Agricultural Economics Review*, Vol. 9, pp. 5-21.

Arrow, K. et al. (1993), "Report of the NOAA Panel on Contingent Valuation", *Federal Register*, Vol. 58, No. 10, pp. 4602-4614, http://www.economia.unimib.it/DATA/moduli/7_6067/materiale/noaa%20report.pdf

Australian Government (2013), *Best Practice Regulation Handbook*. Australian Government, Canberra.

Bateman, I.J. et al. (2011), "Economic Analysis for Ecosystem Service Assessments", *Environmental and Resource Economics*, Vol. 48, pp. 177-218., http://gcpolcc.org/group-hub/ecosystem-services-team/team-pages/ecosystem-services-resources-e-g_reviews-studies-reports.

Bergstrom, J.C. and A. Randall (2010), *Resource Economics: An Economic Approach to Natural Resource and Environmental Policy,* Edward Elgar, Cheltenham, UK and Northampton, MA.

Cameron, T.A. (1992), "Combining Contingent Valuation and Travel Cost Data for the Valuation of Nonmarket Goods", *Land Economics*, Vol. 68, No. 3, pp. 302-317, http://econpapers.repec.org/article/uwplandec/v_3a68_3ay_3a1992_3ai_3a3_3ap_3a302-317.htm

CAO (2008), *Public-Opinion Poll regarding the Role of Food, Agriculture and Rural Areas*, Cabinet Office, Government of Japan (CAO), A Public-Opinion Poll Report in September, 2008, Tokyo. http://www8.cao.go.jp/survey/h20/h20-shokuryou/index.html.

Cooper, T., K. Hart and D. Baldock (2009), *The Provision of Public Goods through Agriculture in the European Union*, report prepared for DG Agriculture and Rural Development, Contract No 30-CE-023309/00-28, Institute for European Environmental Policy, London.

Defra (2013), *England Natural Environment Indicators*, Defra, London.

Defra (2012), *Observatory Monitoring Framework: Environmental impact: Landscape Indicator DF3: Landscape change*, Defra, London.

Defra (2010), *What Nature Can Do for You: A Practical Introduction to Making the Most of Natural Services, Assets and Resources in Policy and Decision Making*, Defra, London.

Defra (2007), *An Introductory Guide to Valuing Ecosystem Services*, Defra, London.

DEFRA/DARD/SG/WAG (2013), *Agriculture in the United Kingdom 2012,* Department for Environment, Food and Rural Affairs, Department of Agriculture and Rural Development (Northern Ireland), The Scottish Government, Rural and Environment Research and Analysis Directorate, Welsh Assembly Government, The Department for Rural Affairs and Heritage.

D'Emden, F.H., R.S. Llewellyn and M.P. Burton (2008), "Factors Influencing Adoption of Conservation Tillage in Australian Cropping Regions", *Australian Journal of Agricultural and Resource Economics*, Vol. 52, No. 2, pp. 169-182, http://econpapers.repec.org/article/blaajarec/v_3a52_3ay_3a2008_3ai_3a2_3ap_3a169-182.htm.

Diamond, P.A. and J.A.Y. Hausman (1994), "Contingent Valuation: Is Some Number Better than No Number?", *Journal of Economic Perspectives*, Vol. 8, No. 4, pp. 45-64.

Environment Agency (EA) (2004), *The State of Soils in England and Wales*, Environment Agency, Bristol.

Ebel, R. (2012), "Soil Management and Conservation", In Osteen, C., J. Gottlieb, and U. Vasavada (Eds.), *Agricultural Resources and Environmental Indicators, 2012 Edition*, US Department of Agriculture, Economic Research Service, Economic Information Bulletin Number 98.

European Commission (2011), *Attitudes of European Citizens towards the Environment*, Special Eurobarometer 365, European Commission, Brussels.

European Commission (2009), *The Europeans in 2009, Special Eurobarometer*, 308/Wave 71.1, European Commission, Brussels.

Fleischer, A. and Y. Tsur (2000), "Measuring the Recreational Value of Agricultural Landscape", *European Review of Agricultural Economics*, Vol. 27, No. 3, pp. 385-398, http://erae.oxfordjournals.org/content/27/3/385.short.

Goulder, L.H. and D. Kennedy (2011), "Interpreting and Estimating the Value of Ecosystem Services," in Kareiva et al. (2011) *Natural Capital: Theory and Practice of Mapping Ecosystem Services*, Oxford University Press, Oxford.

Hall, C., A. McVittie and D. Moran (2004), "What Does the Public Want from Agriculture and the Countryside? A Review of Evidence and Methods", *Journal of Rural Studies*, Vol. 20, pp. 211–225, http://www.researchgate.net/profile/Alistair_McVittie/publication/223059106_What_does_the_public_want_from_agriculture_and_the_countryside_A_review_of_evidence_and_methods/links/0912f511e5e2379622000000.pdf.

Hart, K. et al. (2011), *What Tools for the European Agricultural Policy to Encourage the Provision of Public Goods*, Study for the European Parliament, PE 460.053, June 2011.

Hein, L. et al. (2006), "Spatial Scales, Stakeholders and the Valuation of Ecosystem Services", *Ecological Economics*, Vol. 57, pp. 209-228, http://www.researchgate.net/profile/Ekko_Van_Ierland/publication/222704896_Spatial_scales_stakeholders_and_the_valuation_of_ecosystem_services/links/00b7d53cbed6c30ba1000000.pdf.

Hellerstein, D. et al. (2002), *Farmland Protection: The Role of Public Preferences for Rural Amenities*, Agricultural Economic Report No. 815, Economic Research Service/USDA.

Hodge, I. and M. Reader (2007), *Maximising the Provision of Public Goods from Future Agri-environment Schemes*, Final Report for Scottish Natural Heritage, Rural Business Unit, Department of Land Economy, University of Cambridge, Cambridge.

Howley, P. et al. (2014), "Contrasting the Attitudes of Farmers and the General Public regarding the 'Multifunctional' Role of the Agricultural Sector," *Land Use Policy*, Vol. 38, pp. 248-256, http://ac.els-cdn.com/S0264837713002561/1-s2.0-S0264837713002561-main.pdf?_tid=75e903fc-0b72-11e5-9862-00000aab0f02&acdnat=1433502373_8e9e52a782ae926f0894feb787af6234.

Howley, P., C.O. Donoghue and S. Hynes (2012), "Exploring Public Preferences for Traditional Farming Landscapes", *Landscape and Urban Planning*, Vol. 104, pp. 66-74, http://www.sciencedirect.com/science/article/pii/S0169204611002854.

Hübner, R. and J. Kantelhardt (2010), "Demand for Public Environmental Goods from Agriculture: Finding a Common Ground", Paper presented at the 9th European IFSA Symposium, 4-7 July 2010, Vienna, Austria.

Jones, J., P. Silcock and T. Uetake (2015), "Public Goods and Externalities: Agri-environmental Policy Measures in the United Kingdom", *OECD Food, Agriculture and Fisheries Papers*, No. 83, OECD Publishing, Paris.
DOI: http://dx.doi.org/10.1787/5js08hw4drd1-en.

Keech, W.R., M.C. Munger and C. Simon (2012), "Market Failure and Government Failure", Paper submitted for presentation to Public Choice World Congress, 2012, Miami. Public Version 1.0—2-27-12.

Kling, C.L., D.J. Phaneuf and J. Zhao (2012), "From Exxon to BP: Has Some Number Become Better than No Number?", *Journal of Economic Perspectives*, Vol. 26, No. 4, pp. 3-26, https://www.aeaweb.org/articles.php?doi=10.1257/jep.26.4.3.

Kling, C.L. (1997), "The Gains from Combining Travel Cost and Contingent Valuation Data to Value Nonmarket Goods", *Land Economics*, Vol. 73, No. 3, pp. 428-439.

Kolstad, C.D. (2011), *Intermediate Environmental Economics: International Second Edition*, Oxford University Press, New York.

Land Trust Alliance (2010), *2010 National Land Trust Census Report: A look at Voluntary Land Conservation in America*, Land Trust Alliance. Washington, D.C.

Madureira, L., J.L. Santos, A. Ferreira and H. Guimarães (2013), *Feasibility Study on the Valuation of Public Goods and Externalities in EU Agriculture: Final Report*, A Study Commissioned by European Commission Joint Research Centre, Institute for Prospective Technological Studies Agriculture and life Sciences in the Economy, Contract No. 152423. University of Trás-os-Montes e Alto Douro.

McVittie, A., D. Moran and S. Thomson (2009), *A Review of Literature on the Value of Public Goods from Agriculture and the Production Impacts of the Single Farm Payment Scheme*, Rural Policy Centre Research Report, Report Prepared for the Scottish Government's Rural and Environment Research and Analysis Directorate (RERAD/004/09), SAC, Edinburgh.

Moran, D., A. McVittie, D. Allcroft and D.A. Elston (2007), "Quantifying Public Preferences for Agri-environmental Policy in Scotland: A Comparison of Methods," *Ecological Economics*, Vol. 63, pp. 42-53., http://ac.els-cdn.com/S0921800906005167/1-s2.0-S0921800906005167-main.pdf?_tid=e1722216-0b72-11e5-a046-00000aab0f27&acdnat=1433502554_9efd9d854fa3fdb5dee346eb6feb39b4.

OECD (2013a), *Providing Agri-environmental Public Goods through Collective Action*, OECD Publishing, Paris.
DOI: http://dx.doi.org/10.1787/9789264197213-en.

OECD (2013b), *OECD Compendium of Agri-environmental Indicators*, OECD Publishing, Paris.
DOI: http://dx.doi.org/10.1787/9789264186217-en.

OECD (2012), *Evaluation of Agri-environmental Policies: Selected Methodological Issues and Case Studies*, OECD Publishing, Paris.
DOI: http://dx.doi.org/10.1787/9789264179332-en.

OECD (2010), *Guidelines for Cost-effective Agri-environmental Policy Measures*, OECD Publishing, Paris.
DOI: http://dx.doi.org/10.1787/9789264086845-en.

OECD (2006), *Cost-Benefit Analysis and the Environment: Recent Developments*, OECD Publishing, Paris.
DOI: http://dx.doi.org/10.1787/9789264010055-en.

OECD (2005), *Multifunctionality in Agriculture: What Role for Private Initiatives?*, OECD Publishing, Paris.
DOI: http://dx.doi.org/10.1787/9789264014473-en.

OECD (1999), *Cultivating Rural Amenities: An Economic Development Perspective*, OECD Publishing, Paris.
DOI: http://dx.doi.org/10.1787/9789264173941-en.

OECD (1994), *Agricultural Policy Reform: New Approaches: The Role of Direct Income Payments*, OECD Publishing, Paris.

OECD (1992), *Agricultural Policy Reform and Public goods*, OECD Publishing, Paris.

Olmstead, S. (2010), "The Economics of Water Quality". *Review of Environmental Economics and Policy*, Vol. 4, No. 1, pp. 44–62, http://reep.oxfordjournals.org/content/4/1/44.abstract.

Pagiola, S., K. von Ritter and J. Bishop (2004), "Assessing the Economic Value of Ecosystem Conservation", *Environment Department Papers*, No. 101, The World Bank, Washington D.C.

Pannell, D. and A. Roberts (2015), "Public goods and externalities: agri-environmental policy measures in Australia", *OECD Food, Agriculture and Fisheries Papers*, No. 80, OECD Publishing, Paris.
DOI: http://dx.doi.org/10.1787/5js08hx1btlw-en.

Piperno, S. and W. Santagata (1992), "Revealed Preferences for Local Public goods: The Turin Experiment", in D. King (eds.), *Local Government Economics in Theory and Practice*, Routledge, London.

Ribaudo, M., L. Hansen, D. Hellerstein and C. Greene (2008), *The Use of Markets to Increase Private Investment in Environmental Stewardship*, United States Department of Agriculture, Economic Research Service, Economic Research Report Number 64, Washington D.C.

Rural Investment Support Europe (RISE) (2009), *RISE Task Force on Public Goods from Private Land*, Brussels.

RSPB (2013), *RSPB Facts and Figures*, RSPB, Bedfordshire, www.rspb.org.uk/about/facts.aspx, accessed 23/7/2013.

Sakuyama, T. (2005), *Incentive Measures for Environmental Services from Agriculture: Briefing Note on the Roles of Agriculture Project in the FAO: Socio-economic Analysis and Policy Implications of the Roles of Agriculture in Developing Countries*, Food and Agriculture Publications, Rome.

Saunders, C., G. Greer, B. Kaye-Blake and R. Campbell (2009), *Economics Objective Synthesis Report*, Agricultural Research Group on Sustainability, ARGOS Research Report: No. 09/04, New Zealand.

Schrijver, R. and T. Uetake (2015), "Public goods and externalities: agri-environmental policy measures in the Netherlands", *OECD Food, Agriculture and Fisheries Papers*, No. 82, OECD Publishing, Paris.
DOI: http://dx.doi.org/10.1787/5js08hwpr1q8-en.

Shortle, J. and T. Uetake (2015), "Public Goods and Externalities: Agri-environmental Policy Measures in the the United States", *OECD Food, Agriculture and Fisheries Papers*, No. 84, OECD Publishing, Paris.
DOI: http://dx.doi.org/10.1787/5js08hwhg8mw-en.

Stern, N. (2006), *Stern Review: The Economics of Climate Change*, Cambridge University Press, Cambridge.

Sundberg, J.O. (2006), "Private Provision of a Public Good: Land Trust Membership," *Land Economics*, Vol. 82. No. 3, pp. 353-366.

Turner, R.K., D. Pearce and I. Bateman (1993), *Environmental Economics: An Elementary Introduction*, Johns Hopkins University Press, Baltimore.

UK National Ecosystem Assessment (2011), *The UK National Ecosystem Assessment: Synthesis of the Key Findings*. UNEP-WCMC, Cambridge.

Uetake, T. (2015), "Public goods and externalities: agri-environmental policy measures in Japan", *OECD Food, Agriculture and Fisheries Papers*, No. 81, OECD Publishing, Paris. DOI: http://dx.doi.org/10.1787/5js08hwsjj26-en.

Weimer, D. and A.R. Vining (2010), *Policy Analysis: Concepts and Practice,* 5th Edition, Pearson Education Limited. Harlow.

Chapter 4

Environmental targets and reference levels

This chapter discusses who should bear the costs of providing agri-environmental public goods, and how countries set agri-environmental targets and reference levels. Environmental targets are defined as desired (voluntary) levels of environmental quality that go beyond the minimum requirements or minimum (mandatory) levels of environmental quality for the agricultural sector. Reference levels are defined as the minimum level of environmental quality that farmers are obliged to provide at their own expense. They define the benchmark between avoidance of negative effects and the provisions of positive ones. This chapter presents several examples of environmental targets and reference levels.

Reference level framework

In the case of market failure associated with agri-environmental public goods, in order to secure their provision, some form of public intervention may be needed (Cooper et al., 2009; OECD, 2010a). However, questions remain: to what extent should government intervene? To consider this point, a framework for reference levels is useful (OECD, 2001).

Environmental reference levels are defined as the minimum level of environmental quality that farmers are obliged to provide at their own expense. Environmental targets are defined as desired (voluntary) levels of environmental quality that go beyond the minimum requirements or minimum (mandatory) levels of environmental quality for the agricultural sector in a country (OECD, 2001; 2010a).

Sometimes farmers provide agri-environmental public goods beyond the reference level. In this case the farmer or landowner might be entitled to compensation. When agricultural activities push the level of environmental services below the reference level, then farmers are required to restore the reference level by their own costs (the Polluter-Pays-Principle) (OECD, 1997).

Figure 4.1 illustrates the relationship between environmental targets and reference levels by using four different cases (where X represents the level of environmental quality corresponding to environmental targets [X^T]; reference levels [X^R]; and current farming practices [X^C]). All cases (A to D) represent an identical environmental outcome and allocation of farm resources as the environmental target, X^T, is the same. What differs among these cases is the distribution of costs associated with achieving the defined environmental target (i.e. who pays or who is charged) (OECD, 2001; 2010a).

- ***Case A*** represents a situation where current farming practices provide a level of environmental quality corresponding to a reference level ($X^C=X^R$) above the environmental target (X^T). Thus, farmers are already using the farming practices required for achieving the socially desired environmental outcome. With X^T and X^R achieved at zero opportunity costs, *no policy action* is needed. In such a case, the reference level X^R would normally be achieved through current farming practices X^C ("good farming practices") with costs borne by farmers, and partly by consumers who buy agricultural products.

- ***Case B*** represents a situation where current farming practices (X^C) provide environmental performance below the reference level defined at the level of the environmental target ($X^T=X^R$). In this case, farmers are emitting pollution ($X^C<X^R$), and they need to adopt farming practices required to achieve the desired environmental target level (X^T) *at their own expense* (the Polluter-Pays-Principle). If not, the government may charge a tax or penalty to induce compliance.

- ***Case C*** represents a situation where current farming practices achieve environmental performance corresponding to the chosen reference level ($X^C=X^R$) that is below the target level (X^T). In this case, farmers *may need to be compensated* for changing from current farming practices (X^C) to practices required to achieve the environmental target (X^T).

- ***Case D*** represents a situation similar to Case C, where current farming practices (X^C) provide environmental performance below the environmental target level (X^T), but with the reference level above the environmental performance level of current farming practices (X^C) and below the environmental target (X^T). For improving their environmental performance, farmers need to adopt appropriate farming practices *at their own expense* up to the reference level (X^R) – if not, the government may charge a tax or penalty. Requirements for farmers to further improve their environmental performance beyond X^R to reach the environmental target X^T may need to be remunerated.

Figure 4.1. Environmental targets and reference levels

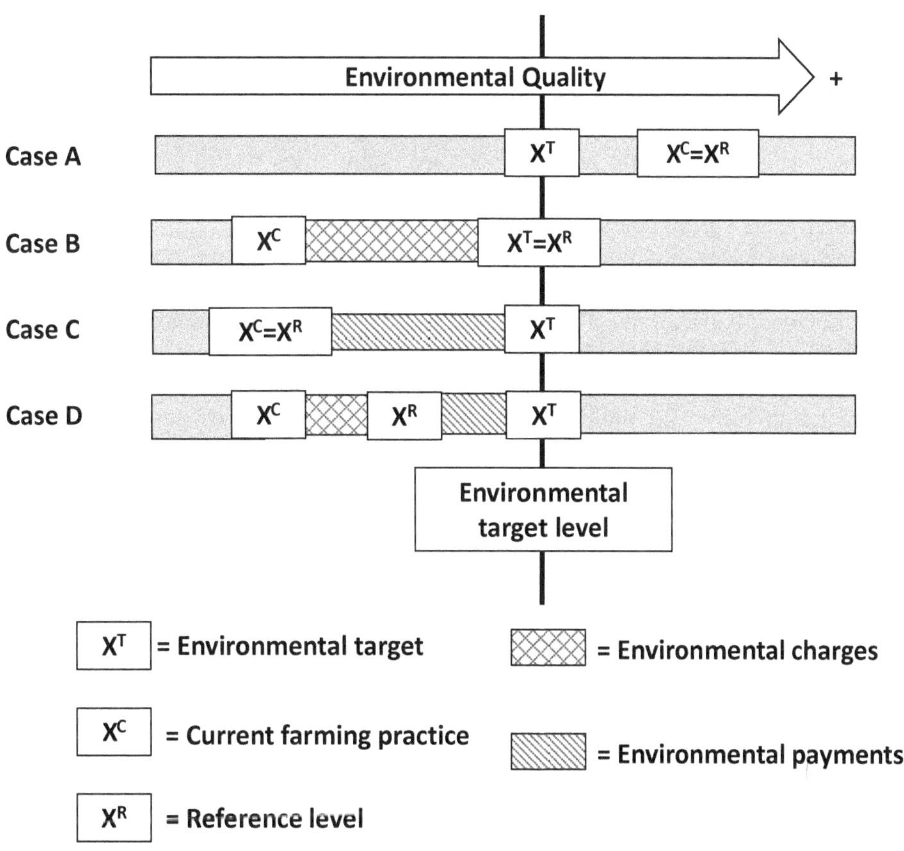

Source: OECD (2001), *Improving the Environmental Performance of Agriculture: Policy options and market approaches*, OECD Publishing, Paris. DOI: http://dx.doi.org/10.1787/9789264033801-en.

It is known that the definitions of environmental targets and reference levels vary between countries (OECD, 2010a); however, there have been few studies which examine how each country defines its environmental targets and reference levels. This book attempts to identify how countries set their reference levels and environmental targets for agri-environmental public goods. This chapter will firstly discuss environmental targets, secondly, reference levels and, lastly, the relationship between property rights and reference levels.

Environmental targets

Setting clear environmental targets for each agri-environmental public good such as biodiversity and water quality is important. Environmental targets are the desired levels of environmental quality that society tries to achieve. Governments, if necessary, provide support to farmers to help them provide an adequate amount of agri-environmental public goods and achieve these environmental targets. Each country sets environmental targets for various agri-environmental goods and some of them are decided as a part of broader environmental issues. For instance, Japan sets Environmental Standards based on Basic Environment Law, which decide the ideal goals of the policies. The Environmental Standards include all sectors, not only agricultural sectors. Currently, Environmental Standards that are related to agriculture are ones for air quality, water quality and soil quality (Uetake, 2015). In EU countries, some strategies or directives (e.g. EU Biodiversity Strategy, EC Water Framework Directive) set overall environmental targets, not just for public goods associated with agriculture (Jones et al., 2015; Schrijver and Uetake, 2015). Environmental targets, ideally, should try to improve the environment; however, keeping current situations could be also environmental targets since many agri-environmental situations keep worsening.

In principle, environmental targets should be output based or directly related to the status of agri-environmental public goods provided. However, through the examination of environmental targets in the studied OECD countries, it becomes clear that environmental targets are not always clearly defined for many agri-environmental public goods. There are many cases where proxy indicators or pressure indicators are used. For instance, Japanese National Biodiversity Strategy 2012-2020 (Japanese Government, 2012) sets various targets about biodiversity including agricultural biodiversity in Japan. The strategy includes 50 quantitative indicators (both agri-environmental and non-agri-environmental indicators). Agri-environmental indicators include ones about farm inputs and practices (e.g. the number of areas where Good Agricultural Practice is introduced, setting withhold standard for pesticide registration for all agricultural pesticides), farm systems (e.g. the number of registered *eco-farmers*, the total number of participants in local collective action) and agricultural infrastructures (e.g. prevention of reducing farmland in hilly and mountainous areas, the percentage of people who have access to agricultural community effluent treatment systems). However, for some of these indicators, it is difficult to find the clear relationships with the outcome, i.e. the status of biodiversity. The Australian main agri-environmental programme, *Caring for Our Country*, sets a number of specific targets, but some of them are targets for proxy indicators and pressure indicators such as the number of farmers adopting management practices to improve soil quality and biodiversity, not directly targeting soil quality and biodiversity (Pannell and Roberts, 2015).

In addition, in some cases, there are no quantitative targets, and instead, qualitative targets are set. For example, maintaining agricultural landscape is an important agri-environmental public good in Japan, the Netherlands and the United Kingdom; however, their targets are often quantitative targets such as keeping agricultural landscape in a certain area which makes it difficult to evaluate policy measures (Jones et al., 2015; Schrijver and Uetake, 2015; Uetake, 2015).

Furthermore, targets of policy measures are often vague. Even if there are overall environmental targets (e.g. preserving biodiversity), it is not always clear to what extent a particular policy measure (e.g. payments for environmentally friendly farming practices) tries to address the targets, and to what extent other policy measures (e.g. technical assistance and extension) try to contribute to achieve the targets (Jones et al., 2015; Schrijver and Uetake, 2015; Uetake, 2015).

Moreover, in some cases, environmental targets are not set. For example, environmental targets on carbon storage are missing in Japan because of lack of appropriate data and knowledge (Uetake, 2015). Environmental targets should be based on generally accepted criteria, such as SMART (Specific, Measurable, Attainable, Realistic and Timely) (OECD, 2010b) and the concept of SMART targets is adopted by some countries such as Australia (Pannell and Roberts, 2015). However, as reviewed, few environmental targets are SMART.

Environmental targets depend on society's preferences for environmental quality (OECD, 2010a). They are decided based on historical and cultural backgrounds, levels of economic development and international treaties, but compared to reference levels, political concerns and interests can be more directly reflected when targets are decided. The efficient setting of environmental targets has to balance the benefits of pursuing agri-environmental objectives against the resulting welfare losses due to lower production or consumption of other goods and services associated with agriculture (OECD, 2010a).

Reference levels

Once environmental targets are set, in order to understand who should bear costs to achieve the targets, it is necessary to decide reference levels. Reference levels define the benchmark between avoidance of negative effects and the provision of positive ones (OECD, 1997). Following the framework of the Figure 4.1, this book applies the reference levels to some of the case study countries. Case A (good farming practices) does not need government intervention, thus, this book focuses on the remaining three cases. There are several examples in the studied OECD countries that belong to Case B (Environmental charges), Case C (Environmental payments) and Case D (Environmental charges and payments).

Case B is where the Polluter-Pays-Principle applies. In this case, to improve the environmental quality, farmers have to bear costs up to a reference level, which is defined at the level of the environmental target ($X^T=X^R$). There are many regulations which require farmers to bear costs to reduce negative impacts on the environment (e.g. pesticide control, water quality control). However, among five country cases examined in this book, there are few cases where the reference level is defined at the level of the environmental target ($X^T=X^R$). An example is air quality control related to nuisance odours and disposal of effluent in Australia. This is managed largely through planning restrictions by locating intensive animal industries away from human population centres on a state-by-state basis (Pannell and Roberts, 2015). In this case, livestock farmers must achieve environmental targets at their own expense. In most cases, beyond the reference level environmental targets are set ($X^T>X^R$), and other policy measures (e.g. environmental payments) are implemented along with environmental charges to meet these.

Case C is where farmers are remunerated for their provision of agri-environmental public goods. This book identifies that most cases of carbon storage apply to this case (e.g. Japan, the Netherlands and the United Kingdom). As carbon storage is a relatively new issue, based on current farming practices ($X^C=X^R$), governments are seeking the way to improve the capacity of carbon storage by promoting the adaption of specific farming practices through environmental payments ($X^T>X^R$).

Some cases of agri-environmental public goods apply to Case D (Environmental charges and payments). For example, some cases of biodiversity apply here. In Australia and the United States, endangered species are regulated and protected by federal and state laws. Some states protect wetlands and native vegetation. Landowners must bear the private opportunity costs of the forgone land uses or of activities to mitigate impacts, which define reference levels for biodiversity. In addition, to further expand and protect biodiversity, these countries provide financial assistance to achieve environmental targets (e.g. Caring for Our Country in Australia; Environmental Quality Incentives Program (EQIP), Conservation Reserve Program (CRP) and Conservation Stewardship Program (CSP) in the United States) (Pannell and Roberts, 2015; Shortle and Uetake, 2015).

Reference levels and technical assistance

In addition to the above four cases identified by OECD (2001), this book identifies where ***Case E*** (Environmental charges and technical assistance) extension services and technical assistance are used instead of agri-environmental payments. What is the relationship between technical assistance and reference levels? Figure 4.2 is a simple model that explains this point. It represents a situation similar to Case D of the Figure 4.1, where current farming practices (X^C) provide environmental performance below the environmental target level (X^T), but with the reference level above the environmental performance level of current farming practices (X^C) and below the environmental target (X^T). To improve their environmental performance, farmers need to adopt appropriate farming practices *at their own expense* up to the reference level (X^R); if not, the government may charge a tax or penalty. This is same for Case D. However, instead of environmental payments, technical assistance is used to further improve such performance by farmers beyond the reference level (X^R) to the environmental target (X^T). Pannell (2008) argues that technical assistance and extension is useful when there are private benefits to farmers as well as public benefits. According to him, even if governments persuade farmers to adopt environmentally friendly farming practices, farmers may not do so if these practices require farmers to bear additional costs.

For example, water quality on point source pollution associated with agriculture in Japan is represented by Case E. To meet the reference levels set by the Water Pollution Control Law, livestock farmers are obliged to meet the requirements to prevent water pollution bearing the costs. However, environmental targets on water quality are set beyond this reference level by the Environmental

Standards based on the Basic Environment Law. The Environmental Standards are the ideal level for protecting human health and preserving the environment in Japan, and they are administrative goals. Currently, to achieve the goals on water quality, technical assistance and extension services are mainly adopted to promote voluntary activities of farmers to enhance water quality[1] (Uetake, 2015).

Figure 4.2. Environmental charges, technical assistance and reference levels

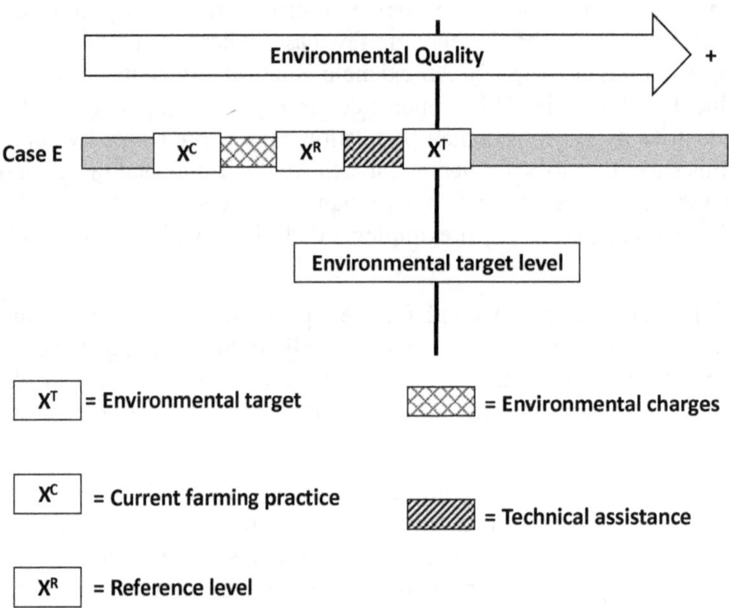

Regarding the reference levels, it is important to examine two points: 1) how reference levels are achieved and 2) how they are set.

As Figure 4.1 illustrates, reference levels are achieved by current farming practices (Case A and C), or environmental charges (Case B and D), not by environmental payments, since costs to meet reference levels are borne by farmers by definition. In considering policy design, regulations and cross compliance are particularly important.

Reference levels and regulations

Farmers are often required to achieve reference levels by meeting regulations. Typically, regulation levels and reference levels are equal and farmers adopt the necessary treatment to mitigate the negative impacts on the environment (***Case F*** of Figure 4.3). However, reference levels are not always equal to regulation levels. In some cases, regulation levels are set beyond current farming practices to improve the environment, and for which governments may provide some transitional support including payments. For instance, in Japan, the Netherland, and the United Kingdom, to mitigate environmental problems associated with livestock and improve water, soil and air quality, farmers are required to install suitable facilities to store livestock manure and slurry. Relevant governments provide technical advice and assistance, and in some cases provide financial assistance, to help farmers meet the enhanced standards (Jones et al., 2015; Schrijver and Uetake, 2015; Uetake, 2015). In this case, regulation levels are set beyond the reference levels so that costs for meeting regulation levels are borne by society (***Case G-1*** of Figure 4.3). However, it must be noted that these government support should be transitory and the reference level should be increased up to the regulation levels gradually (***Case G-2*** of Figure 4.3).

Figure 4.3. Reference levels and regulation levels

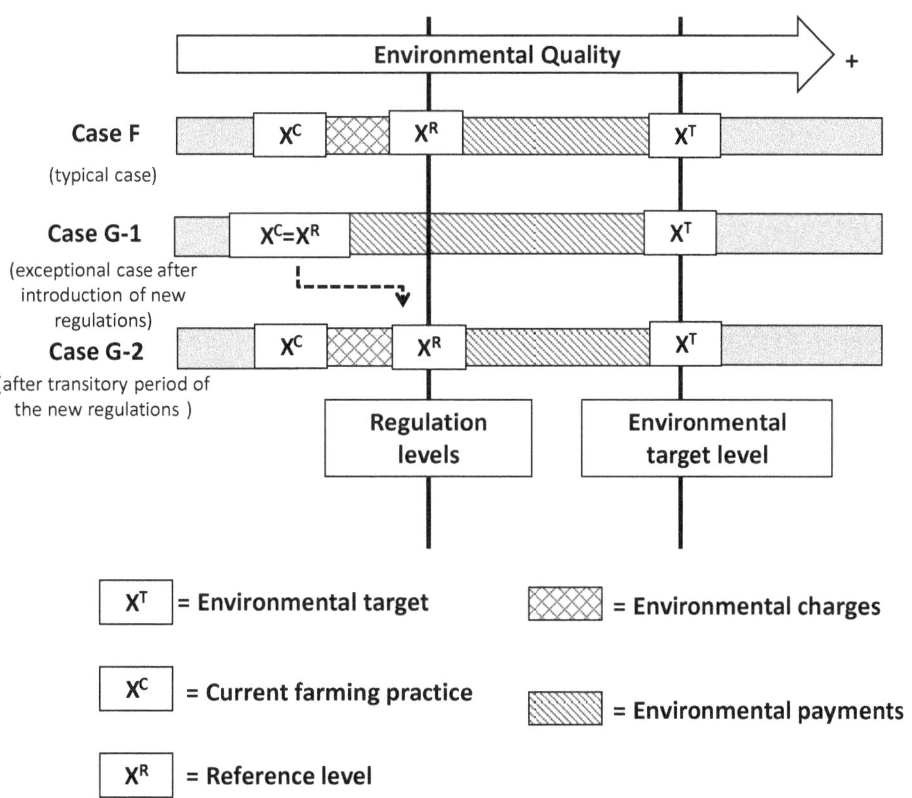

Reference levels and cross-compliance

Cross compliance is a number of conditions related to *environmental* performance that farmers are required to meet in order to be eligible to receive an *agricultural income support payment*. It provides a link between one or more policy instruments (OECD, 2010c).

For instance, the United States was the first OECD member country to introduce cross-compliance measures. Cross-compliance is used for addressing soil conservation (Sodbuster) and wetland protection (Swampbuster). For example, for addressing soil conservation and protecting soil quality, farmers who produce annually tilled agricultural commodity crops on highly erodible cropland have to adopt adequate erosion protection (X^R) if they voluntarily enter into a contract with the government on most agricultural income support payments (***Case H*** of Figure 4.4). Farmers who seek conservation payments such as EQIP, CSP and CRP must first meet compliance requirements throughout their farm without assistance from Federal agri-environmental payments (***Case I*** of Figure 4.4) (Shortle and Uetake, 2015; OECD, 2010c).

Figure 4.4. Reference levels and cross compliance: Highly erodible land conservation in the United States[1]

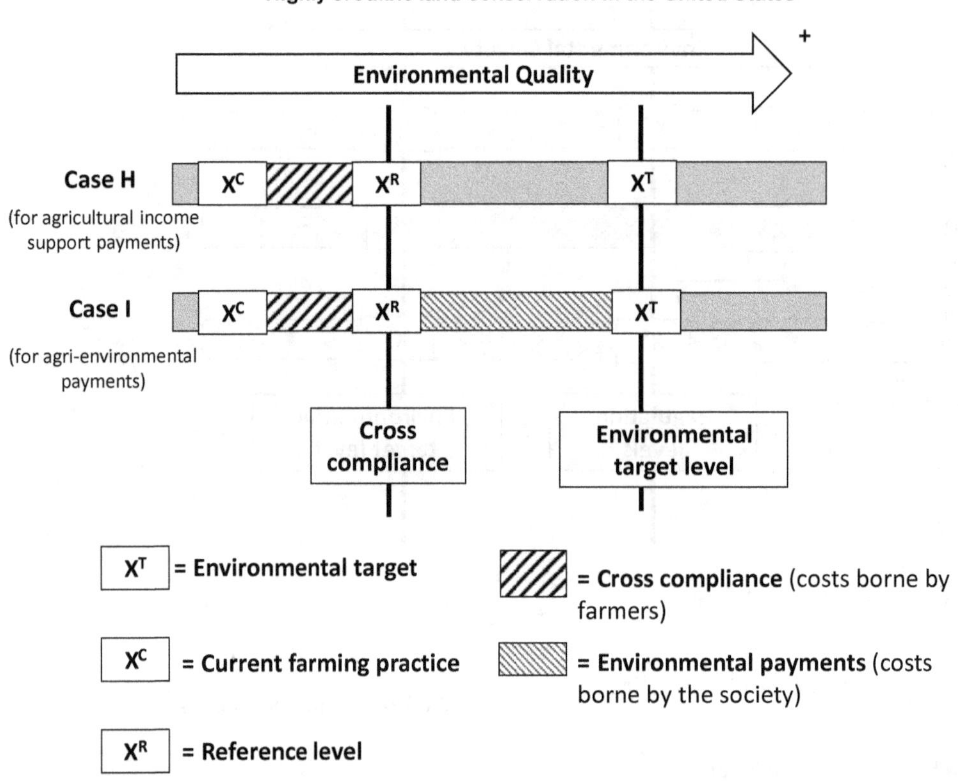

The relations among cross compliance, reference levels and payments vary depending on the country and the targeted agri-environmental public goods (OECD, 2010c).

How are reference levels set?

This book examined reference levels in the studied countries and identified that some reference levels are clearly defined, but others are not clearly defined or tacit. For instance, there are both specified environmental targets and reference levels for water quality and soil quality in Japan. For these public goods, reference levels were set when pollution from various industries became problems in 1960-70s. Not only farmers but also other business operators are obliged to meet requirements to prevent pollution. Minimum regulations are generally set by acts based on scientific evidence (e.g. water quality) (Uetake, 2015).

On the other hand, some agri-environmental public goods such as carbon storage have no clearly set reference levels in Japan, the Netherlands and the United Kingdom (Jones et al., 2015; Schrijver and Uetake, 2015; Uetake, 2015). This does not mean that there are no reference levels. It means that current farming practices are generally the reference levels (Case C of Figure 4.1).

Reference levels may also be set in terms of the driving forces (e.g. farm inputs and practices) or the environmental outcome (i.e. agri-environmental public goods) (OECD, 2010c). Table 4.1 summarises how reference levels are set in terms of the driving forces and environmental outcomes in the case of the Netherlands. As shown in the table, most reference levels are set in terms of driving forces such as farm inputs management (e.g. pesticides and fertiliser management). Among the studied OECD countries, reference levels that are set in terms of environmental outcomes were not found for some agri-environmental public goods such as air quality and resilience to natural disasters. This may be because controlling environmental outcomes by farmers is difficult for these agri-environmental public goods and asking them to bear costs for something that they cannot fully control is generally difficult to reach social consensus.

Reference levels at various scales are another issue. In some cases, it could be better to define reference levels at regional or local scales, rather than at national scales. For instance, the Landscape Act in Japan promotes the development of landscape plans including the agricultural landscape by communities. Local citizens and farmers decide their future plans for conserving landscape. They decide where to and how to conserve landscape through promoting environmentally friendly farming. Environmental targets and reference levels on agricultural landscape are set at local scales, not at national scales in Japan (Uetake, 2015).

Table 4.1. Reference levels in terms of driving forces and environmental outcomes: An example from the Netherlands

Agri-environmental public goods[1]	Reference levels: Driving forces (farm inputs and practices, agricultural infrastructure)	Reference levels: Environmental outcomes (agri-environmental public goods)
Soil protection and quality	• Soil management practices, restriction on applying farm inputs, stubble management, green manure crops, under grazing control, sewage sludge control and regulation on nitrate vulnerable zones	-
Water quality	• Soil management practices, restriction on applying farm inputs, establishment of no spread zones and regulation on nitrate vulnerable zones	• Nitrogen runoff control
Water quantity/availability	• Water licencing	• Water table and abstraction control
Air quality	• Soil management practices, burning control, sewage sludge control and regulation on nitrate vulnerable zones • Pollution prevention and control for intensive industrial agricultural units (mainly pigs and poultry)	-
Climate change – greenhouse gas emissions[2]	-	-
Climate change – carbon storage[2]	-	-
Biodiversity	• Habitats/special area protection • Grazing and burning control • Environmental impact assessments	• Wild birds protection
Agricultural landscapes	• Conservation of hedges, rows of trees and other landscape features	-
Resilience to natural disasters	• Managing dykes and irrigations	-

1. As explained in Chapter 1, these goods are not always public goods. Sometimes, they can be private goods (e.g. agricultural landscape with use value by visitors can be a private good if exclusion can be made) or when they cause harm, they can be defined as private bads or public bads (Kolstad, 2011). Careful examination on whether these goods have characteristics of non-rivalry and/or non-excludability is necessary for each case.
2. For climate change (greenhouse gas emissions and carbon storage), current farming practices are equal to reference levels.

Source: Adapted from Schrijver and Uetake (2015), *Public Goods and Externalities: Agri-environmental Policy Measures in the Netherlands*, and Hart, K. et al. (2011), *What Tools for the European Agricultural Policy to Encourage the Provision of Public goods*.

Changing reference levels over time

Reference levels can change over time as well. For instance, management of irrigation systems had been done by farmers by their own costs in Japan. At that time, the reference level and the level of current farming practices coincided and they were above the environmental target level (X^R=X^C>X^T) (***Case J-1*** of Figure 4.5). However, because of the decreased number of farmers and aging, the level of farming practices decreased and it became difficult to manage the irrigation systems (X^R>X^T>X^C) (***Case J-2*** of Figure 4.5). Thus, to maintain irrigation systems and secure the provision of associated agri-environmental public goods such as water availability, flood prevention and biodiversity, Japan decided to provide payments to local communities composed of farmers and non-farmers that manage irrigation systems to achieve this environmental target. In this case, the reference level lowered (X^T>X^R=X^C) (***Case J-3*** of Figure 4.5). This could be explained from the demand side. Previously, the common perception of the irrigation systems was that they were mainly for farmers, and non-farmers or local communities did not appreciate their value, at least explicitly. However, as the importance of the environment associated with the irrigation systems started to be recognised more widely, society and local communities were asked to bear some of the costs for the maintenance as beneficiaries of the services.

Figure 4.5. Changing reference levels: An example of a Japanese irrigation system and associated agri-environmental public goods

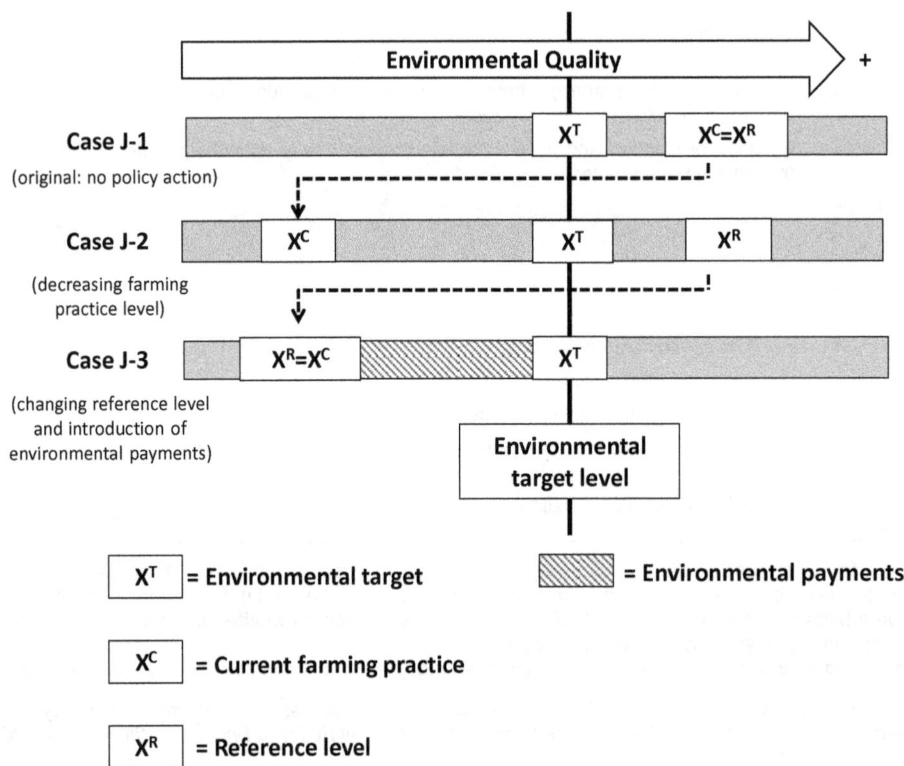

Efforts for enhancing reference levels

Some countries try to enhance reference levels beyond the minimum standards or regulated constraints. For instance, in Australia, there are a number of Acts and regulations relating to agri-environmental public goods, such as regulations on limiting farmer's ability to clear vegetation for their agricultural production in order to protect biodiversity (***Case K-1*** of Figure 4.6). In addition, Australia adopts the Duty of Care approach and Codes of Practices as voluntary approaches to ask farmers to take care of the environment and bear some of the costs for improving the environment (***Case K-2*** of

Figure 4.6). However, these approaches are totally voluntary without financial assistance, as a result, their current usage is limited (Pannell and Roberts, 2015) as is their effectiveness.

Figure 4.6. Efforts for enhancing reference levels: An example from Australia

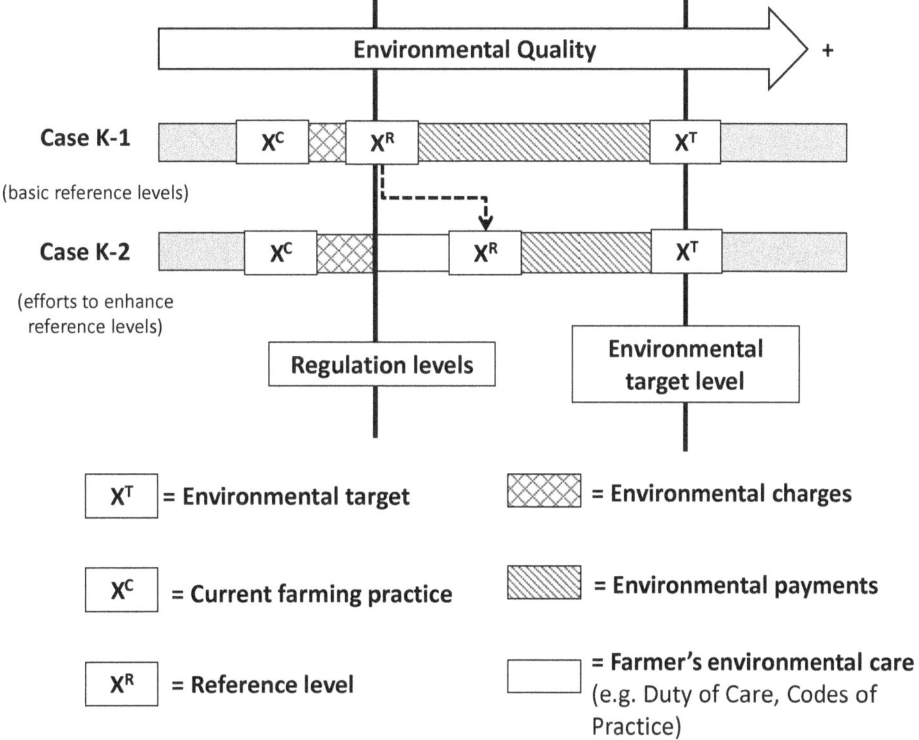

Introducing new regulations usually means enhancing reference levels. As discussed in the Figure 4.3, new regulation levels are sometimes set beyond current farming practices to improve the environment and which farmers must undertake at their own expense. Many environmental regulations such as water and air quality control were introduced in the 1970s, and these regulations pushed the reference levels higher.

Reference levels after achieving environmental targets

If farmers and society in general achieve environmental targets, careful examination on continued government intervention is necessary (Figure 4.7). Current farming practices achieve environmental performance corresponding to the chosen reference level ($X^C=X^R$), that is below the target level (X^T). To achieve the environmental target, an environmental payment is introduced (***Case L-1*** of Figure 4.7) and farmers gradually start to adopt environmentally-friendly farming practices which provide a level of environmental quality corresponding to the environmental target ($X^C= X^T$) (***Case L-2*** of Figure 4.7). Thus, governments may decide to increase the reference level up to the environmental target and may stop providing the environmental payments (***Case L-3*** of Figure 4.7). However, in this case, it should be examined whether it is possible to keep maintaining environmental quality as set as the environmental target without continuous government intervention. If governments stop government support, farmers may have difficulty in maintaining the environmental target and therefore decrease the environmental quality level of farming practices (***Case L-4*** of Figure 4.7). Even if it is necessary to continue providing government support, policy approaches may need to change. Typically speaking, improving environmental quality and maintaining environmental quality or preventing the deterioration of environmental quality need different approaches and solutions. Keeping the old policy measures for improving environmental quality may bring larger policy and administrative costs than would additional benefits, so that governments may need to modify the policies to maintain the environmental quality or prevent the deterioration of the environmental quality (***Case L-5*** of Figure 4.7). In some cases, society wants to improve environmental quality further and sets a higher environmental goal than the original one. In this case, governments may need to keep providing environmental payments to improve the environment (***Case L-6*** of Figure 4.7).

Figure 4.7. Reference levels after achieving an environmental target

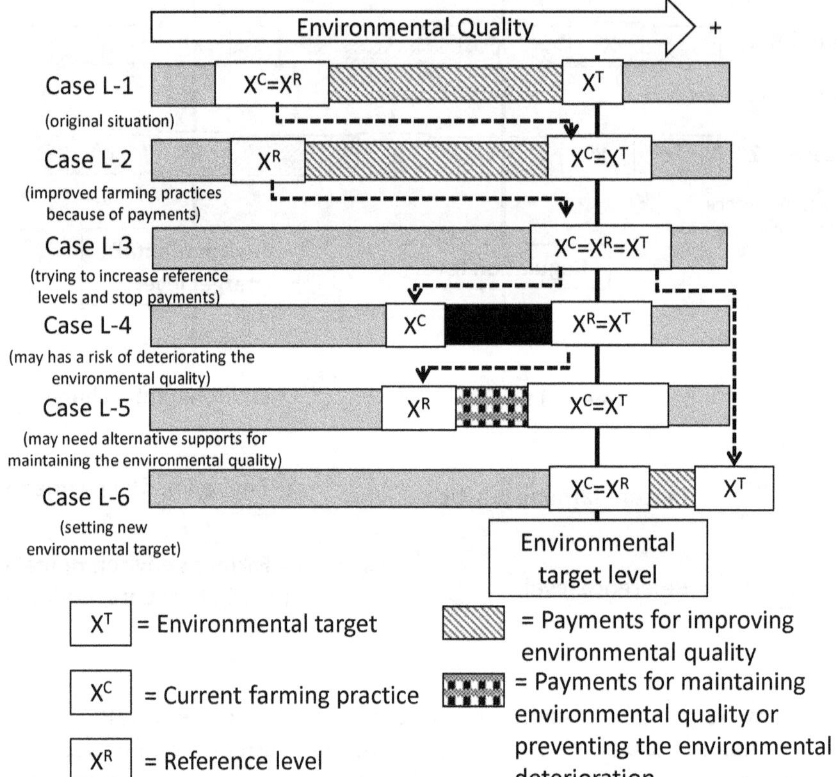

Reference levels and beneficiaries of agri-environmental public goods

Governments play the major role in deciding the level of reference levels and distribution of costs associated with agri-environmental public goods. In addition, the distribution of costs associated with agri-environmental public goods is decided indirectly by the beneficiaries such as local communities. In many cases the provision of agri-environmental public goods benefits or imposes costs on particular individuals (OECD, 1992). Especially when they occur at a local scale, it is easy to identify beneficiaries. In this case, they should bear some of the costs involved for quality gains above reference levels (the Beneficiary-Pays-Principle) (OECD, 1996; Defra, 2013). Some community-based approaches to manage and provide agri-environmental public goods (e.g. the Caring For Our Country in Australia, Measures to Conserve and Improve Land, Water, and the Environment in Japan) are examples since both farmers and non-farmers participate in collective action and provide assistance for providing agri-environmental public goods, i.e. sharing some of the supply costs (OECD, 2013) (***Case M*** of Figure 4.8). Beyond the reference level (X^R), some costs are borne by communities.

Figure 4.8. Reference levels, beneficiaries and cost burden sharing

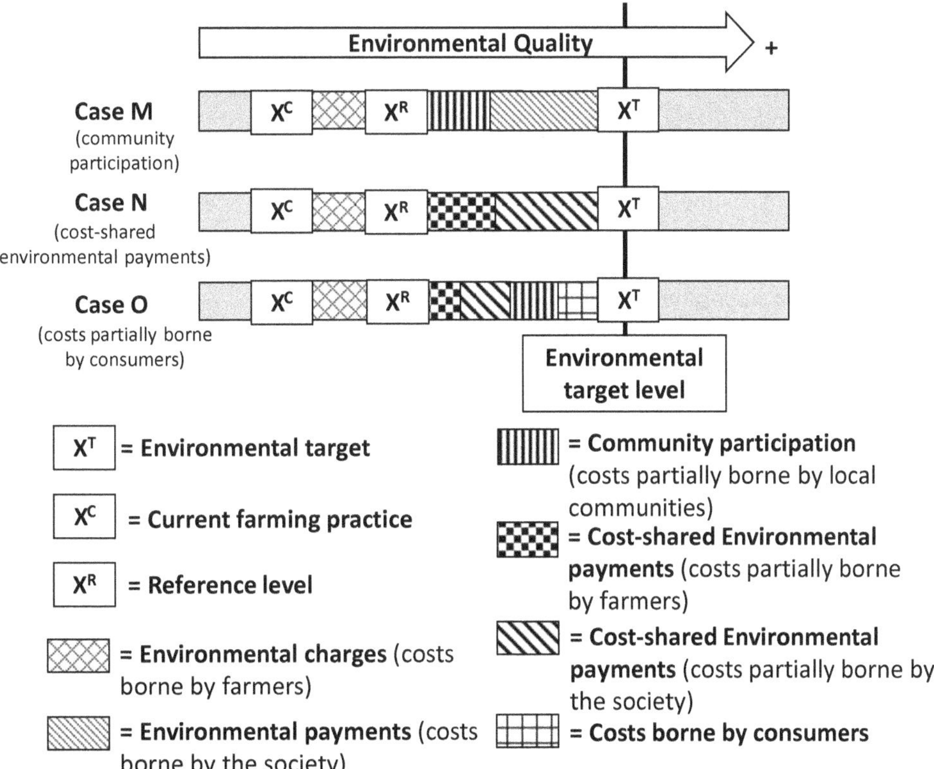

Some agri-environmental public goods also bring benefits to farmers. For example, better soil quality brings both private benefits to farmers (e.g. higher productivity) and public benefits to society (e.g. prevention of soil erosion, carbon storage and biodiversity). In these cases, beyond the minimum level of environmental quality that farmers are obliged to provide at their own expense (X^R), farmers should bear some of the additional costs. Governments may use cost-shared environmental payments to ask farmers to bear additional costs. In this case, participating farmers must cover some additional costs by themselves (***Case** N* of Figure 4.8). Examples include the Environmental Quality Incentives Program (EQIP) in the United States (Shortle and Uetake, 2015). To what extent farmers share costs depend on benefits enjoyed by farmers.

Costs borne by consumers have not been addressed in this book. In many cases, consumers bear some of the costs for the provision of agri-environmental public goods when purchasing food. For example, labelling can help consumers to understand how food is produced and some will pay additional costs to purchase food grown in an environmentally friendly way (RISE, 2009).[2] Typically these agri-environmental public goods bring direct benefits to farmers and local communities. Thus, as shown in ***Case O*** of Figure 4.8, if community participation and cost-shared environmental payments are introduced taking into account the costs borne by consumers, the actual amount of environmental payment that governments need to implement to achieve the environmental target level can be considerably smaller than those assumed in Case D of Figure 4.1. Depending on the distribution of benefits, the appropriate burden of costs varies so that identifying and measuring costs and benefits among different groups of people is significant (OECD, 1992).

Where should reference levels be set?

As discussed, this book provides several cases of reference levels which provide a useful tool to examine who should bear the costs of providing agri-environmental public goods. However, in the OECD case study countries, reference levels and environmental targets are not always clearly defined. More discussion on reference levels and environmental targets are necessary.

Identifying demanders and suppliers of agri-environmental public goods is a first step to discussing the distribution of burdens. Some principles, such as the Polluter-Pays-Principle and the Beneficiary-Pays-Principles, and approaches, such as cost-sharing and community participation, can help how to set reference levels and allocate the burdens among different groups. Although the economic and environmental aspects are important issues to be taken into consideration, it is also important that social aspects such as the equity of the distribution of economic costs and benefits between and among different groups (farmers, consumers and taxpayers) are also considered (OECD, 2010a). Policy makers need to weigh the trade-offs between environmental effectiveness, economic efficiency, other benefits and costs (including administrative costs), and equity and income distribution in deciding these reference levels.

Administrative procedures for deciding reference levels are set by, for example in the United Kingdom and the Netherlands, the government and/or relevant authorities, and informed by international and EC commitments and policies, based on scientific evidence, expert analysis and public consultation. For many agri-environment public goods, this process takes place in the context of Rural Development Programmes (RDPs) for the countries of the Common Agricultural Policies (CAP) (Jones et al., 2015; Schrijver and Uetake, 2015). In Japan, councils composed of experts are usually held and after sharing their draft targets with the public, their comments are taken into consideration and reference levels decided. When setting minimum standards that farmers are obliged to meet, discussions are based on scientific evidence. Although the overall framework is generally set by Japanese laws, concrete targets are often set in administrative documents (Uetake, 2015).

Environmental reference levels are based on distribution (equity) considerations, historical and cultural backgrounds, historical social preferences, levels of economic development (developing countries may have lower reference levels than developed countries because of population, poverty and hunger), levels of pollution, international treaties, and property rights (OECD, 2010a; 2010c). In particular, property rights are important factors which affect reference levels.

Reference levels and property rights

Property rights play a significant role. When land property rights have priority over societal claims for certain agri-environmental public goods (e.g. soil and water quality, biodiversity), the pursuit of environmental objectives may infringe on such rights and may require compensation (OECD, 2010c). If, however, property rights are assigned to consumers or to society, farmers have to compensate them for losses associated with their agricultural activities (not only pollution, but also poor quality and scarce quantity of the provision of agri-environmental public goods).

Reference levels may be legally defined by property rights, which entail obligations such as maintenance of the banks of a river or preserving an historic building. Reference levels may be agreed tacitly as well (OECD, 1999).

It is often difficult to determine who holds the property right regarding agri-environmental public goods. While the property rights to land and its tenants are often clearly established, ownership does not always mean that owners take responsibility for the related agri-environmental public goods. For example, the owner of land along a river is not entitled to do whatever he/she wishes with the water because the community may have rights over the water quality and quantity in watercourses. In this case, the ownership of the land and the property right to the water quality and quantity do not belong to same entity (OECD, 1999).

Property rights can change over time because of different social objectives and priorities regarding agri-environmental issues, and different degrees of economic development and population density (Colby, 1995; OECD, 1999, 2001). The conditions under which farmers are rewarded or charged for their environmental performance evolve accordingly. The setting of property rights and reference levels involves complex issues of cultural tradition, equity and efficiency (OECD, 2001; 2010a).

In any case, defining how to take into account the environmental impacts of agriculture and sharing the cost burdens among stakeholders requires a case-by-case response in relation to the settings of the environmental targets and the definition of environmental reference levels. This should be based on the identifying existing property rights so as to define who can ask for remuneration and who is liable for charges (OECD, 2001; 2010a). Box 4.1 provides examples of property rights and reference levels in the OECD case study countries.

Once environmental targets and reference levels are set, policy intervention may be necessary. In the next chapter, policy measures for agri-environmental public goods in the studied OECD countries are reviewed.

Box 4.1. Property rights and reference levels: Examples from selected OECD countries

Australia

Australia has made extensive use of markets for the allocation of water amongst agricultural producers. Water trading allows scarce water resources to be transferred to their most efficient and productive uses. The result has been the generation of significant opportunities to achieve sustainable and efficient water use. The Australian experience is underpinned by a suite of institutional and property right reforms that have made it easier to set up viable water markets. State governments set legislations to make it clear that water is controlled by the State for the public (OECD, 2010d). Farmers are required to have water rights for using water. Since water rights are held by other farmers, if a farmer wants to use more water, he/she needs to purchase the water right from others by his/her own costs. In this case, the reference level is set in terms of driving forces, i.e. water licensing. For successful water markets, generally, several factors are required, including a secure statutory basis for water entitlements; trading rules that reflect hydrological realities; systems for limiting and managing adverse third-party impacts; and robust trading platforms and accounting systems. Although there are many challenges in terms of technical, political, social, cultural and managerial aspects, water markets are well established and are broadly supported by stakeholders and governments in Australia (Pannell and Roberts, 2015).

Japan

In Japan, *satoyama* landscapes (*human-influenced natural environments)* (Box 2.1) are considered to be of national importance. However, property rights of farmland are held entirely by farmers. They do not have obligation to maintain *satoyama* landscapes. Some farmlands have been converted to urban use, or some have been abandoned. As a result, some landscapes are being difficult to be maintained. Since farmers have property rights, in this case, reference levels are set at current farming practices. To preserve *satoyama* landscapes, some regions have introduced *tanada* (terraced paddy fields) ownership system. Beneficiaries of landscapes (citizens who care about the maintenance of the landscape) become "owners" of small parcels of *tanada*. Although actual property rights remain in hands of farmers, citizens pay annual fee to farmers who maintain *tanada* and help farmers keep *tanada* and *satoyama* landscapes. Farmers are remunerated since they do their efforts to conserve landscapes beyond the level that they are obliged to achieve by their own cost.

United States

In the United States, historically, no property rights were set for discharges to water with the result that water was an open access good for pollution. Polluters did not need to bear costs for discharging waste water. As a result, serious degradation of water resources occurred. In 1972, to address this problem, the Unites States enacted the Clean Water Act (CWA) for water quality management. By introducing this CWA, the United States essentially nationalized access to surface waters for point sources of pollution. Since property rights are set for the water, polluters of point sources (animal feeding operations) are required to acquire discharge permits in order to have access to water for discharging waste water. To meet reference levels defined by property rights on the water, polluters of point sources (animal feeding operations) have to bear costs. However, agricultural nonpoint pollution is largely exempted from regulations and most farmers are paid to reduce pollution (Shortle and Uetake, 2015).

Notes

1. There are a few environmental payment programmes which partly address water quality improvement, such as Act on the Appropriate Treatment and Promotion of Utilization of Livestock Manure. But the main objective of this programme is to address livestock environmental problems such as odours and contribute to better soil quality through the utilisation of livestock manure.

2. Asking consumers to cover costs can be controversial in terms of equity. Higher price food can be regressive for socially disadvantaged groups such as the poor.

References

Colby, B.G. (1995), "Bargaining Over Agricultural Property Rights", *American Journal of Agricultural Economics*, Vol. 77, pp. 1186-1191.

Cooper, T., K. Hart and D. Baldock (2009), *The Provision of Public goods through Agriculture in the European Union*, report prepared for DG Agriculture and Rural Development, Contract No 30-CE-023309/00-28, Institute for European Environmental Policy, London.

Defra (2013), *Payments for Ecosystem Services: A Best Practice Guide*, Defra, London.

Hart, K., D. Baldock, P. Weingarten, B. Osterburg, A. Povellato, F. Vannie, C. Pirzio-Biroli and A. Boyes (2011), *What Tools for the European Agricultural Policy to Encourage the Provision of Public Goods*, Study for the European Parliament, PE 460.053, June 2011.

Japanese Government (2012), *National Biodiversity Strategy 2012-2020: Roadmap for Achieving Rich Nature-coexisting Society*, Japanese Government, Tokyo.

Jones, J., P. Silcock and T. Uetake (2015), "Public Goods and Externalities: Agri-environmental Policy Measures in the United Kingdom", *OECD Food, Agriculture and Fisheries Papers*, No. 83, OECD Publishing, Paris.
DOI: http://dx.doi.org/10.1787/5js08hw4drd1-en.

Kolstad, C.D. (2011), *Intermediate Environmental Economics: International Second Edition*, Oxford University Press, New York.

OECD (2013), *Providing Agri-environmental Public Goods through Collective Action*, OECD Publishing, Paris.
DOI: http://dx.doi.org/10.1787/9789264197213-en.

OECD (2010a), *Guidelines for Cost-effective Agri-environmental Policy Measures*, OECD Publishing, Paris.
DOI: http://dx.doi.org/10.1787/9789264086845-en.

OECD (2010b), *Evaluating Development Co-operation: Summary of Key Norms and Standards*, OECD, Paris, http://www.oecd.org/development/evaluation/dcdndep/41612905.pdf.

OECD (2010c), Environmental Cross Compliance in Agriculture, OECD, Paris, http://www.oecd.org/tad/sustainable-agriculture/44737935.pdf.

OECD (2010d), *Sustainable Management of Water Resources in Agriculture*, OECD Studies on Water, OECD Publishing, Paris.
DOI: http://dx.doi.org/10.1787/9789264083578-en.

OECD (2001), *Improving the Environmental Performance of Agriculture: Policy options and market approaches*, OECD Publishing, Paris.
DOI: http://dx.doi.org/10.1787/9789264033801-en.

OECD (1999), *Cultivating Rural Amenities: An Economic Development Perspective*, OECD Publishing, Paris.
DOI: http://dx.doi.org/10.1787/9789264173941-en.

OECD (1997), *Environmental Benefits from Agriculture: Issues and Policies*, OECD Publishing, Paris.

OECD (1996), *Amenities for Rural Development: Policy Examples,* OECD Publishing, Paris.

OECD (1992), *Agricultural Policy Reform and Public goods*, OECD Publishing, Paris.

Pannell, D. (2008), "Public Benefits, Private Benefits, and Policy Intervention for Land-use Change for Environmental Benefits", *Land Economics*, Vol. 84, No. 2, pp. 225-240.

Pannell, D. and A. Roberts (2015), "Public goods and externalities: agri-environmental policy measures in Australia", *OECD Food, Agriculture and Fisheries Papers*, No. 80, OECD Publishing, Paris.
DOI: http://dx.doi.org/10.1787/5js08hx1btlw-en.

Rural Investment Support Europe (RISE) (2009), *RISE Task Force on Public Goods from Private Land*, Brussels.

Schrijver, R. and T. Uetake (2015), "Public goods and externalities: agri-environmental policy measures in the Netherlands", *OECD Food, Agriculture and Fisheries Papers*, No. 82, OECD Publishing, Paris.
DOI: http://dx.doi.org/10.1787/5js08hwpr1q8-en.

Shortle, J. and T. Uetake (2015), "Public Goods and Externalities: Agri-environmental Policy Measures in the the United States", *OECD Food, Agriculture and Fisheries Papers*, No. 84, OECD Publishing, Paris.
DOI: http://dx.doi.org/10.1787/5js08hwhg8mw-en.

Uetake, T. (2015), "Public goods and externalities: agri-environmental policy measures in Japan", *OECD Food, Agriculture and Fisheries Papers*, No. 81, OECD Publishing, Paris.
DOI: http://dx.doi.org/10.1787/5js08hwsjj26-en.

Chapter 5

Policy measures for the delivery of agri-environmental public goods

This chapter analyses the policies implemented to provide agri-environmental public goods and which agri-environmental public goods they target. Many policy measures target multiple agri-environmental public goods, and each agri-environmental public good is targeted by multiple policy measures. However, it is not always clear to what extent a particular policy measure tries to address agri-environmental issues, and the extent to which other policy measures do so. It therefore discusses the importance to target factors that affect the provision of agri-environmental public goods to improve the cost-effectiveness of policy measures.

Overview of the agri-environmental policy measures

Various agri-environmental policy measures such as environmental standards or regulations, environmental taxes, tradable permits and agri-environmental payments are implemented for providing agri-environmental public goods in OECD countries. The characteristics of agri-environmental policy measures are discussed and synthesised by *Guidelines for Cost-effective Agri-environmental Policy Measures* (OECD, 2010a). Box 5.1 summarises several agri-environmental policy measures based on previous OECD studies.

Table 5.1 summarises which agri-environmental policy measures are implemented in the studied OECD countries.[1] It provides an overview of the policy measures.

Table 5.1. Measures addressing environmental issues in agriculture[1]

Measure / country	Australia	Netherlands	Japan	United Kingdom	United States
Regulatory measures					
Regulatory Requirements	XXX	XXX	XX	XX	X
Environmental taxes/charges	NA	X	NA	NA	NA
Environmental cross-compliance[2]	NA	XXX	XX	XX	XX
Financial incentives					
Payments based on farming practices	X	XXX	XXX	XXX	XXX
Payments based on land retirement	NA	X	X	X	XXX
Payments based on farm fixed assets	NA	X	X	X	X
Payments based on outcomes/ performance rankings	NA	NA	NA	NA	X[3]
Tradable rights/permits	X	X	X	X	X
Community based measures	XX	X	NA	NA	NA
Facilitative measures					
Technical assistance and extension	XX	XX	XX	XX	XXX

Note: NA – not applied or marginal; X – low importance; XX – medium importance; XXX – high importance.

1. The importance of the policy instruments in this table is related to the mix of the specific country. It is not designed to compare the importance of specific measures across countries.

2. Environmental cross-compliance may be characterised as de-facto regulatory requirements for farmers that are eligible for agricultural support payments (Vojtech, 2010).

3. In the United States, the Conservation Stewardship Program (CSP) uses a points system to determine a conservation performance ranking that is used to select applicants and determine payment levels. It is important, however, to note that the performance assessment of the CSP is not based on actual environmental outcomes, but on established scoring tables indicating the relative environmental benefit impact of different practices (Shortle and Uetake, 2015).

Source: OECD Secretariat based on Vojtech, V. (2010), "Policy Measures Addressing Agri-environmental Issues", DOI: http://dx.doi.org/10.1787/5kmjrzg08vvb-en.

Table 5.1 does not provide details on which policy measures are used for which agri-environmental public goods, nor has this been done in previous OECD studies. The objectives of agri-environmental policy are often easy to state in general terms but difficult to define and measure precisely. Moreover, some policies address several objectives at the same time, either because objectives are interconnected or because a change in a farm activity can have multiple effects. Each policy measure is discussed in the country case studies (Jones et al., 2015; Pannell and Roberts, 2015; Schrijver and Uetake, 2015; Shortle and Uetake, 2015; Uetake, 2015), and general characteristics of the policy measures are discussed and synthesised in *Guidelines for cost-effective agri-environmental policy measures* (OECD, 2010a). Thus, the analyses here focus on targeting, multiple objectives and policy mixes in order to draw policy implications for better policy design for the provision of agri-environmental public goods.

Box 5.1. Agri-environmental policy measures

Environmental standards regulate producer choices (input standards) or measures of non-market outputs (performance standards). *Input standards* place mandates on driving forces such as the production process, technology, the products that are used, or the manner in which they are used. *Performance standards* regulate polluting emissions from non-agricultural point sources. While input standards do not provide producers with the flexibility or incentives to look for cost-effective solutions to environmental problems, performance standards allow producers to meet mandated requirements in ways of their own choice. Therefore, performance standards in general allow farmers to achieve the standards at a lower cost (OECD, 2010a).

Environmental taxes can be used to reduce negative externalities from agriculture as well as to increase positive externalities (e.g. by reducing tax when producing them). Taxes can be used to internalise, or reduce, the costs of externalities. The concept of the polluter-pays-principle (PPP) is also important. The PPP is the principle by which the polluter bears the cost of measures to reduce pollution, according either to the extent of the total damage done to society or when acceptable levels of pollution have been exceeded (OECD, 2001). When applying the PPP, negative externalities should be taxed so as to generate a socially optimal level of production (OECD, 2011).

Cross-compliance mechanisms are measures requiring farmers to fulfil specific environmental requirements or levels of environmental performance in order to be eligible for agricultural income support payments (OECD, 2010a, 2010b; Vojtech, 2010).

Agri-environmental payments can be used to promote the supply of agri-environmental public goods. If a fixed-rate payment does not consider the heterogeneity in farmers' compliance costs or the site-productivity of agri-environmental public goods, this payment might not be cost-effective. However, targeting the individuals who produce these goods could reduce this problem (OECD, 2010a). Although it is difficult to design a payment system for tackling the problem because of asymmetric information, *auctions* could be useful as they induce farmers to reveal their estimated compliance costs or their net pay-offs via their auction bids. Auctions could thus reduce farmers' information rents and improve the cost-effectiveness of agri-environmental payment schemes (OECD, 2010a). More generally, an incentive-compatible mechanism should be embedded in policy design so as to make individuals reveal information truthfully.

Tradable permits can achieve environmental targets at a lower social cost than traditional environmental standards. Trading can offer a mechanism for allocating environmental effort among those concerned in a cost-effective way even if environmental regulators do not know the abatement costs of individual agents (OECD, 2010a).

Community based measures are policy measures for promoting collective action by farmers and non-farmers through the provision of technical assistance and agri-environmental payments. Collective action can leverage resources among participants and manage or provide agri-environmental public goods at a larger scale that cannot be done by individual farmers. Although most agri-environmental policy measures usually target individual farmers, some OECD countries adopt policy measures specifically target collective action (OECD, 2013).

Technical assistance provides farmers with on-farm information and technical assistance to plan and implement environmentally friendly farming practices (Vojtech, 2010).

Targeting environmental objectives in agriculture

Targeting policies towards precise objectives and tailoring measures to precise needs is expected to achieve a better result with lower transfers than broad-based, non-targeted, policies. A targeted policy only provides transfers in pursuit of specific objectives to specific spatially defined areas and specific farm types (OECD, 2007a; 2008). Environmental targeting channels funding to those areas where the benefits from agri-environmental public goods are greatest relative to the costs of the provision. Targeting can, however, result in an uneven distribution of funding and raises equity concerns (Claassen et al., 2001).

Targeting is a key concept because providing agri-environmental public goods must take into consideration heterogeneity of farmers and agri-environmental public goods; this includes taking into account the different types and the level of complexity and scale of the public goods concerned. For example, if a fixed-rate payment, which is widely offered in many OECD countries, does not consider the heterogeneity in farmers' compliance costs or the site-specificity of agri-environmental public goods, such payment might not be a cost-effective way to encourage farmers to adopt more environmentally-friendly farming practices and provide agri-environmental public goods. These targets could be better met by prioritising zones and farmers who produce such goods (OECD, 2010a).

OECD (2012a) establishes three types of targeting associated with agri-environmental policies:

- *spatial targeting*, relating to the geographical extent and zones in which schemes are to be developed and implemented;
- *structural* targeting, relating to specific farm types or systems to be covered;
- *targeting specific environmental objectives or features* to be protected or managed through the scheme.

The provision of the agri-environmental public goods is affected by three main driving forces: farm systems, farm inputs and practices, and agricultural infrastructure (Figure 2.2). Figure 5.1 synthesises the links between targeting and these driving forces and policy measures in a simple stylised way.

Figure 5.1. Agri-environmental policy measures and targeting

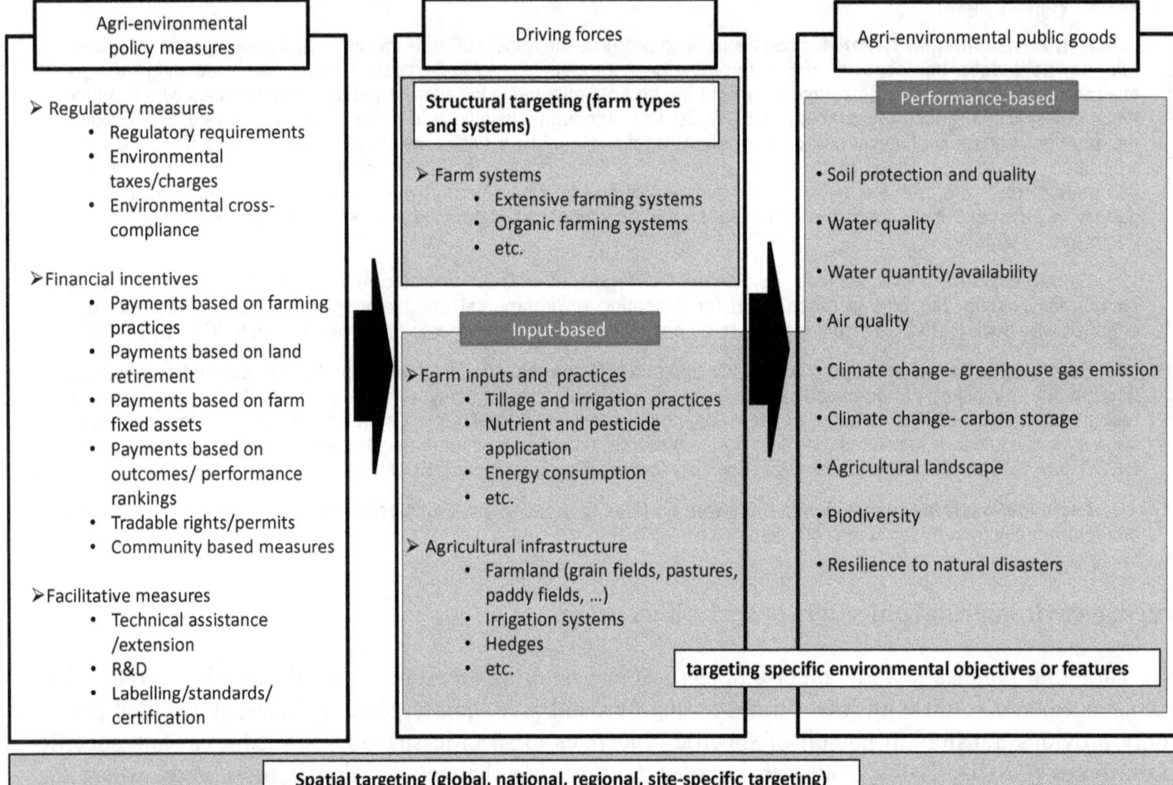

Note: Other non-agri-environmental policies (e.g. agricultural income support payments, risk management policies, trade policies), markets (e.g. commodity markets, supply chain, economy, technology) and other sectors also affect the environmental conditions and agri-environmental public goods. In this very simple figure, only agri-environmental policies and agri-environmental public goods are included.

Spatial targeting

First, it is necessary to consider to whom policy measures apply and by whom policy measures are designed and implemented. One aspect of this question is the geographic region to which the instrument applies (*spatial targeting*) (OECD, 2010a). The choice here depends on the geography of the environmental problem to be solved. Market failures that justify a policy intervention are often locally or regionally confined. Examples of regional interventions are areas with a special environmental interest (e.g. Natura 2000 sites in the European Union) or regions with a specific environmental problem (e.g. nitrogen surplus) (OECD, 2008). In this case, local governments generally play an important role in the design and implementation of policies (OECD, 2006).

Some agri-environmental public goods (e.g. climate change) are global or transnational (Madureira et al., 2013). In this case, central or federal governments play an important role and internationally co-ordinated approaches may be necessary (OECD, 2006). In many cases, the environmental results of policy measures depend on both the size of the targeted areas and the spatial pattern of the areas. Fragmented or distributed areas do not have the same ecological impact as aggregated areas with the same size (Bamière et al., 2013). Thus, spatial targeting needs to consider both size and the spatial configuration of the targeted areas as well as the appropriate level of government responsible for the design of the policy measures.

Structural targeting

Second, it is necessary to consider who within the geographic region should be targeted (*structural targeting*) (OECD, 2010a). This question concerns farming sectors, farm systems and types of farm (OECD, 2012a). Farm systems vary markedly and may have different approaches to agri-environmental policies depending on their perceived impacts on farm management (OECD, 2012a). For example, some policy measures specifically target livestock farmers or organic farmers to improve the environment.

Box 5.2. An example of targeting collective action in the Netherlands

Biodiversity is one of the most important public goods provided by regional farming co-operatives in the Netherlands. The Water, Land & Dijken (WLD), the province of North Holland and other non-governmental parties, such as farmers, volunteers and conservation organisations, work collectively to preserve grassland birds in Laag Holland (Lower Holland). This scheme is implemented by the WLD close to farms, thus substantially increasing the uptake. For example, the WLD signs individual contracts with participating farmers to selectively cut and re-distribute part of the payments they receive from the National Paying Agency. This "skimmed" budget is used for result-oriented payments (according to the number of nests protected) and for private conservations contracts, especially where last-minute measures are concerned. For example, when a field is to be mowed but still densely populated with birds, the WLD can agree with the farmer to postpone mowing.

The European Commission's proposals for the CAP 2014-2020 include a new formal position for collective action, mentioning "groups of farmers" as potential applicants and beneficiaries under the agri-environmental part of the proposals for rural development. The proposals also mention broader possibilities for EU support for co-operative actions, including for organisational costs. The WLD is pleased with these possibilities and is now formulating ideas for the following.

- The practical implementation of these new possibilities.
- Extending the role of regional co-operatives to first pillar CAP payments (direct payments), where 30% of the budget is reserved for environmental measures. Co-operatives could also play an important role in developing an effective "collective delivery."

Source: OECD (2013), *Providing Agri-environmental Public Goods through Collective Action.* DOI: http://dx.doi.org/10.1787/9789264197213-en.

Whether to target individual farmers or groups of farmers is another issue. Agri-environmental policies often apply to individual farmers but some measures address groups of farmers, farmers' representatives or co-operatives, or local collective actions by farmers and non-farmers. Policies that target collective action are especially useful for providing agri-environmental public goods that cannot be provided by individual farmers separately with any significant value, i.e. threshold agri-environmental public goods (Sakuyama, 2005; OECD, 2008, 2013). For public goods that need landscape-scale management, activities by individual farmers may not convert potential goods into valued ones (OECD, 2013). Even if farmers adopt environmentally-friendly farming practices, if these are not co-ordinated at an appropriate scale, it is difficult to achieve a socially optimum level of provision. Landscape-scale management is necessary (Goldman et al., 2007; OECD, 2013; Cong et al., 2014), and some countries try to identify good policy measures for landscape-scale management (e.g. Dutch collective action (Box 5.2), EU-funded CLAIM project[2]). Farmer behaviour is also affected by neighbouring farmers. Taking into consideration both economic factors and non-economic factors — such as habits, cognitions, norms and cultures — is also important to design appropriate agri-environmental policies (OECD, 2012b). Depending on the characteristics of agri-environmental public goods, it may vary whether it is more effective to be provided by individual farmers or by communities.

The environmental effects from agriculture largely depend on the types of farms. For example, Uetake and Sasaki (2014) examined agri-environmental policy measures and their impacts on different types of farms (business and semi-business farm household in plains and mountainous areas) in Japan and showed that semi-business farm household in mountainous areas bring about relatively larger environmental damages. If a fixed-rate payment, which is widely offered in many OECD countries, does not consider the heterogeneity in farmers' compliance costs or the site-specificity of agri-environmental public goods, this payment might not be cost-effective. Targeting the individuals who produce these goods could reduce this problem (OECD, 2010a).

Targeting specific environmental objectives or features

Lastly, *targeting specific environmental objectives or features* to be protected or managed need to be examined. Selecting appropriate target variables is a fundamental issue in designing effective agri-environmental policy measures. Agri-environmental policy measures are broadly differentiated as being based on environmental outcomes (performance-based) or based on farmers' input and technology choices (input-based or practice-based). Performance-based measures emphasis ends or results (agri-environmental public goods) while input-based measures emphasise means (driving forces) (OECD, 2010a).

Input-based instruments may directly regulate the levels or characteristics of farm inputs that affect the provision of agri-environmental public goods (e.g. pesticides, fertilisers, fuels), prescribe the specific farm practices that affect the flow of agri-environmental public goods (e.g. specific technologies used, such as nutrient or pesticide best-management practices) or require farmers to manage agricultural infrastructures (e.g. irrigation systems). Performance-based instruments focus on the flow of agri-environmental public goods from the farm, such as water quality (nutrient runoff) or soil quality (sediment erosion) (OECD, 2010a). Performance-based measures can provide flexibility to farmers to select farming practices that are least cost in the context of each farm and address the heterogeneity of farm conditions and the supply of environmental services (OECD, 2010a). Table 5.2 summarises the key points of input-based and performance-based instruments. Only a few performance-based instruments exist in the studied countries due to the difficulties of designing such instruments; Box 5.3 gives a snapshot of a pilot case in Australia.

A precise measurable definition of the targeted policy objective and the units by which it will be measured are important. For example, agri-environmental policy objectives can be measured in monetary units (e.g. costs, benefits or the difference between costs and benefits), in non-monetary units (e.g. number of hectares of wetlands preserved), or as ratios (e.g. greenhouse gas emissions per square meter or emissions per kg of output) (OECD, 2008).

As a general rule, targets should be close to the desired outcomes as much as possible, given the limits determined by monitoring requirements, technical knowledge and administrative feasibility. The more remote the target is from the desired objective, the more risks exist regarding unintentional side-effects and leakages of transfers, and the less likely the targeted objective is to be achieved (OECD, 2008).

Table 5.2. Input-based instruments and performance-based instruments

	Input-based instruments	Performance-based instruments
Targeting	**Means (driving forces)**	**Ends (agri-environmental public goods)**
Targeting variables	• Farm practices • Farm inputs (pesticides, fertilisers, fuels etc.) • Agricultural infrastructure (irrigation system, hedges etc.) • Etc.	• Water quality (nutrient runoff) • Soil protection and quality (sediment erosion) • Etc.
Examples	• First-generation environmental policies for air and water quality protection (i.e. those enacted in the late 1960s and 1970s) such as the US Clean Water Act and Clean Air Act. These policies included bans on some pesticides, and regulations governing uses and practices for others.	• Policy measures targeting performance estimated by annual average gross soil loss (soil protection and quality), estimates of nutrient surplus (water quality), and estimates of carbon being sequestered under various practices (carbon storage).
Advantages	• Easier to develop and can be the only feasible option.	• Gives farmers flexibility to choose the means, for which they will have incentives to do so at the minimum cost.
Problems	• Limit the flexibility of farms to choose cost-effective options. • Reduced efficiency. • Risk of failure to achieve environmental objectives due to the focus on means rather than ends.	• Uncertainty. The regulator is unable to observe or measure farmers' contributions to many agri-environmental public goods. • Lack of appropriate data or proxies. • Difficulty of designing policies.

Source: Adapted from OECD (2010a), OECD (2010), *Guidelines for Cost-effective Agri-environmental Policy Measures*, DOI: http://dx.doi.org/10.1787/9789264086845-en.

Box 5.3. Targeting, auctions and performance-based instruments: An example from Victoria, Australia

Significant amount of remaining native vegetation, which provides habitat for various threatened species, exist in private lands in the State of Victoria in Australia. Much of these private lands is small scale, spatially dispersed and of variable conservation significance.

In order to preserve the native vegetation, the State of Victoria started the BushTender programme in 2001, evolving into a larger scheme, EcoTender. These programmes use a reverse auction to achieve biodiversity outcomes with private landholders. Farmers choose land management practices necessary for the biodiversity management and make bids. Government purchases biodiversity management actions based on the biodiversity significance and the expected improvement in habitat due to landholder management.

This auction system helps to address the information asymmetry issues and target farmers that can effectively address biodiversity issues. Farmers understand how participation in conservation activities will affect their production and profit motives. On the other hand, environmental experts often have greater knowledge of the value of the environmental assets occurring on private lands. This auction system tries to reveal the hidden information held by both parties, and bring better environmental performance in a cost-effective way.

In addition, the State of Victoria launched an outcome-based BushTender pilot project in 2009-10. Although farmers usually agree on practices (input-based instrument), in this pilot project farmers are required to meet certain biodiversity outcomes to maintain the values of biodiversity on their lands (performance-based instrument). If farmers meet the cover and diversity of native plants requirement on the site, they are eligible to receive payments. The State of Victoria will compare both input-based and performance-based BushTender projects after finishing the period of the pilot project in 2014.

Source: Pannell. D. and A. Roberts (2015), "Public Goods and Externalities: Agri-environmental Policy Measures in Australia", and Department of Environment and Primary Industries, State Government Victoria (www.dse.vic.gov.au/conservation-and-environment/biodiversity/rural-landscapes/bushtender).

Targeting and transaction costs

Targeting brings the possibility of larger benefits in a cost-effective way than broad-based non-targeted policies. However, targeted policies usually have higher transaction costs than non-targeted policies. Costs include those incurred by governments and other agencies in gathering information, planning and designing policies, collecting revenue, and monitoring and checking the outcome of policies. They also include the cost incurred by farmers when transacting with the government, as well as when obtaining information on policies and claiming benefits (OECD, 2007a, 2007b; Claassen et al., 2008). Transaction costs occur at all stages of policy implementation, from policy design and enactment to final evaluation, through interactions between and within government agencies, private organisations and programme participants (OECD, 2007b). Therefore, reducing transaction costs as a result of targeting is a crucial aspect in policy design and choice. These costs can be reduced by sharing experiences across agencies, regions or countries, exploiting already existing administrative networks, integration of government and private information systems, reducing the number of agencies, and through the use of information technologies (OECD, 2007b). Trust-building can also reduce the transaction costs (Dunn, 2011).

Generally speaking, the information and data to properly measure and monitor transaction costs are lacking, thus data is necessary to control and reduce such costs (OECD, 2007b). The gains from targeting need to be weighed against the potential increase in administrative and other transaction costs of the programme, as well as equity considerations (OECD, 2010a).

Multiple objectives and targeting

Some policies address several objectives at the same time. Ribaudo et al. (2008) and Ribaudo (2013) developed a matrix of agricultural conservation/environmental problems, policy instruments and Federal programmes in the United States. Referring to their matrix, this book develops the matrices which explain which policy measures target which objectives (some policy measures target several objectives) (Annex Table A1-A.5). These tables are useful to identify what kinds of policy measures are implemented for targeting which agri-environmental public goods and how certain policy measures try to target multiple objectives.

Complex links between policy measures and objectives

Many policy measures are implemented in OECD countries, and the links between these policy measures and their objectives are complicated. First, in order to provide a sense of this complicated linkage between policy measures and agri-environmental public goods, Table 5.3 selects some policy measures from the studied countries and compares their targeted agri-environmental public goods.

Generally speaking, this book finds that many regulatory requirements and tradable permits target single objectives (e.g. water quality, soil protection and quality, air quality), while other measures target multiple objectives.

Pollution is caused by various economic activities, not only by farming activities, and it is necessary to cover all sectors to prevent pollution (e.g. water pollution, air pollution). In addition, it is often easier to regulate outputs, rather than regulating various practices of different sectors (e.g. regulating point sources of water pollution is easier than regulating thousands of practices by various industries). Sometimes, it is necessary to regulate the absolute levels of the outputs for human health and the environment (e.g. drinking water regulation). Thus, it appears natural for regulatory measures to target single objectives.

On the other hand, financial incentives and facilitative measures often target farm inputs, farming practices and related agricultural infrastructures. These driving forces affect the provision of a wide range of agri-environmental public goods such as biodiversity and water quality. Therefore, if policy measures target these drivers, as a result, policy measures tend to target multiple objectives.

Table 5.3. Selected examples of policy measures and targeted agri-environmental public goods

Types of policy measures	Programme	Targeted agri-environmental public goods[1] and number of those public goods	
Regulatory requirements	Agricultural Land Soil Pollution Prevention Law (JPN)	Soil protection and quality	1
	Clean air act (USA)	Air quality	1
	Clean Water Act (USA)	Water quality	1
Environmental taxes/charges	Water board districts levy (NLD)	Water quality/availability, agricultural landscape	2
Environmental cross-compliance	Cross compliance (GBR)	Agricultural landscapes, biodiversity, water quality, water quantity/availability, soil protection and quality, resilience to fire	6
Payments based on farming practices	Direct Payments to Farmers in Hilly and Mountainous Areas (JPN)	Soil protection and quality, water availability, biodiversity, agricultural landscapes, resilience to flooding	5
	Environmental Stewardship (GBR)	Agricultural landscapes, biodiversity, water quality, soil protection and quality, climate change (greenhouse gas emissions, carbon storage), resilience to flooding	6
Payments based on land retirement	England Woodland Grant Scheme (GBR)	Agricultural landscapes, biodiversity, water quality, climate change (carbon storage), resilience to flooding	5
Payments based on farm fixed assets	Environmental tax reduction programmes (NLD)	Biodiversity, climate change (greenhouse gas emissions, carbon storage), air quality	3
Payments based on outcomes	Conservation Stewardship Program (USA)	Soil protection and quality, water quality, wetlands, biodiversity, air quality	4
Tradable rights/permits	Water markets (AUS)	Water quantity/availability	1
	Wetlands Mitigation Banking (USA)	Wetlands	1
Community based measures	Caring For Our Country (AUS)	Water quality, farmland biodiversity and native vegetation, soil protection/soil protection and quality	3
	Measures to Conserve and Improve Land, Water, and the Environment (JPN)	Water quality, water availability, biodiversity, agricultural landscapes, resilience to flooding, snow damage and fire	5
Technical assistance/extension/ R&D/labelling/standards/certification	Farming Advice Service (GBR)	Agricultural landscapes, biodiversity, water quality, water quantity/availability, climate change (greenhouse gas emissions, carbon storage)	5

1. As explained in Chapter 1, these goods are not always public goods. Sometimes, they can be private goods (e.g. agricultural landscape with use value by visitors can be a private good if exclusion can be made) or when they cause harm, they can be defined as private bads or public bads (Kolstad, 2011). Careful examination on whether these goods have characteristics of non-rivalry and/or non-excludability is necessary for each case.

Some patterns of multiple objectives

Policy measures targeting farm systems

Policy measures often target farm systems, for example those geared towards improving the livestock environment. Since 1999, the Japanese government has implemented a set of policy measures under the Act concerning Appropriate Treatment and Promotion of Utilisation of Livestock Manure (AATPULM) to address environmental issues associated with livestock. Regulatory standards have been set for manure management. National and local governments finance facilities that recycle farm waste so as to help farmers meet a mandatory standard for livestock manure management. AATPULM addresses environmental problems such as odours (air quality) and water quality, and contributes to better soil protection and quality through the utilisation of livestock manure (Uetake, 2015) (Figure 5.2).

Figure 5.2. Policy measures targeting farm systems in Japan: An example of multiple objectives

Agri-environmental policy measures
- AATPULM
  - Regulatory standards for livestock manure
  - Payments for recycling facilities
  - Guidelines for livestock manure management

Driving forces
- Farm systems
  - Livestock farming systems

Agri-environmental public goods
- Water quality
- Soil quality
- Air quality

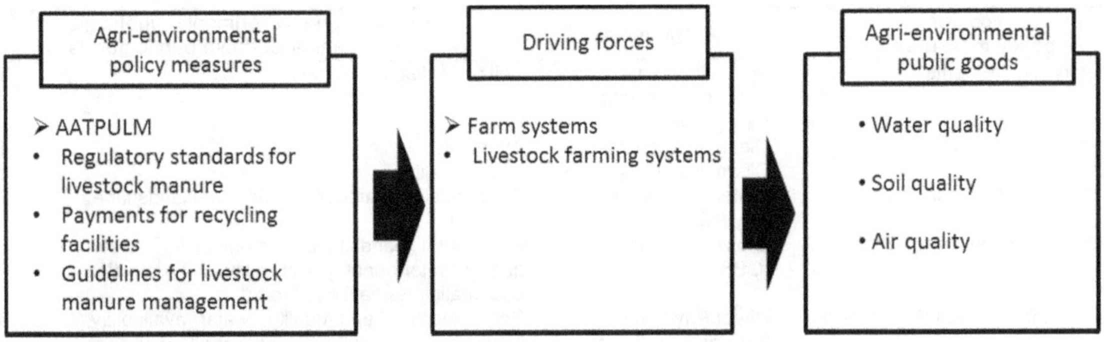

AATPULM: Act concerning Appropriate Treatment and Promotion of Utilisation of Livestock Manure.

Policy measures targeting farm practices

Most agri-environmental policies target specific (well-defined and controlled) management practices which are intended to provide agri-environmental public goods over and above a reference level (Vojtech, 2010). The Environmental Stewardship (ES) Scheme in England is such an example. It operates at two levels: Entry and Higher. The Entry Level is based on a set payment on a per hectare basis. Points are amassed from a menu of good environmental practices aimed mostly at biodiversity and wildlife. The Higher Level goes above and beyond Entry Level, i.e. all Higher Level agreements must have an Entry Level component. Payments are still based on a menu of options with fixed standard payments. But the payments are actual and not via a points system and there is no fixed or upper limit on an area basis other than those set by the EU payments regulations. The range of activities is much wider and more tailored to specific situations and habitats (e.g. parkland trees or chalk downland native flora). Aims are broader and more ambitious. These aims have been nuanced to particular target areas. Thus, for example, habitat for particular bird species or traditional landscape features that are native to the area or important archaeological protection will be favoured. There are also more options within historic features and landscape and soil and water protection than would be the case at Entry Level (Jones et al., 2015) (Figure 5.3). It is generally considered to be the case that farmers tend not to participate in policy measures for delivering agri-environmental public goods that require a significant change of farm practices. Thus, farmer involvement in the design of the policy scheme helps to ensure larger participation of farmers in the scheme (Barreiro-Hurlé et al., 2010).

Figure 5.3. Policy measures targeting farm practices in the United Kingdom: An example of multiple objectives

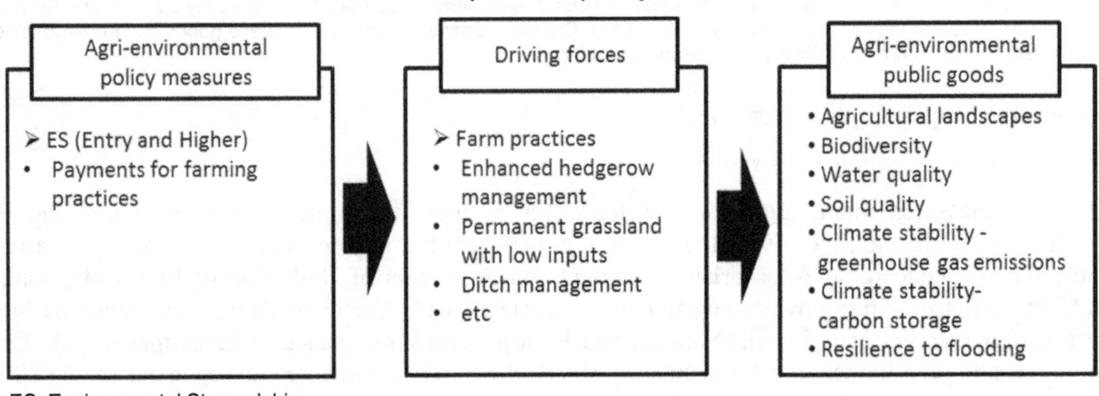

ES: Environmental Stewardship.

Policy measures targeting farm inputs

Some policy measures target farm inputs. For example, the Act for the Establishment and Extension of Agricultural Practices that Facilitate the Sustainable Development of Agriculture (SDA) in Japan improve soil quality and water quality through the reduction of the use of chemical fertilisers and pesticides. Under this Act, the certification system of "Eco-farmers" was established and financial support (interest-free loans) is made available for certified "Eco-farmers" who introduce facilities to improve farming practices (Uetake, 2015) (Figure 5.4).

Figure 5.4. Policy measures targeting farm inputs in Japan: An example of multiple objectives

Agri-environmental policy measures
➢ SDA
• Payments (interest-free loans) for facilities
• Certification systems

Driving forces
➢ Farm inputs
• Reducing the use of chemical fertilisers and pesticides by half compared to conventional farming

Agri-environmental public goods
• Water quality
• Soil protection and quality

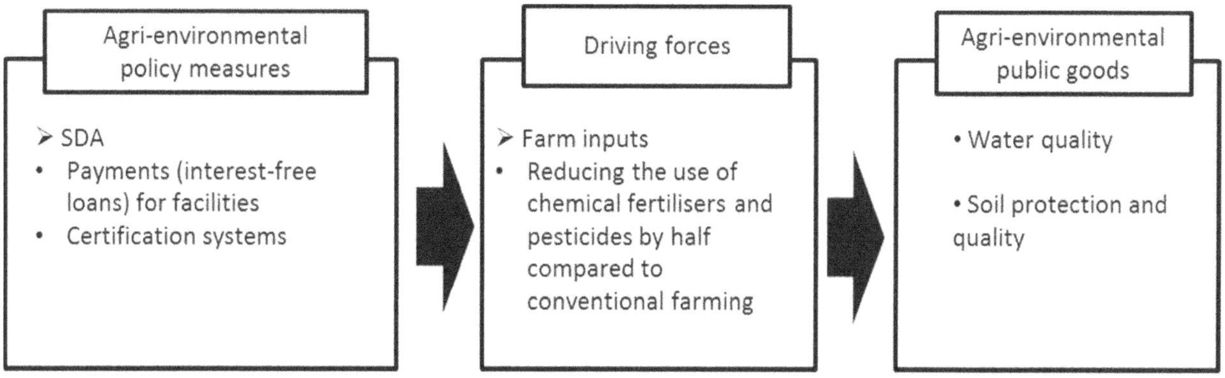

SDA: Sustainable Development of Agriculture.

Policy measures targeting agricultural infrastructure

Not only agriculture, but also agricultural infrastructure (e.g. farmland, irrigation systems, hedges) also provide various agri-environmental public goods. For example, in the United States, there are several land retirement programmes that target cropland. The biggest land retirement programmes is the Conservation Reserve Program (CRP). The government pays landowners if they remove land from production and plant buffers, grass or trees, or restore wetland condition. Through the conversion of cropland to grassland or forest, this programme creates wildlife habitat and restores wetlands (biodiversity), reduces soil erosion and contributes to soil, water and air quality (Shortle and Uetake, 2015) (Figure 5.5).

Figure 5.5. Policy measures targeting agricultural infrastructure in the United States: An example of multiple objectives

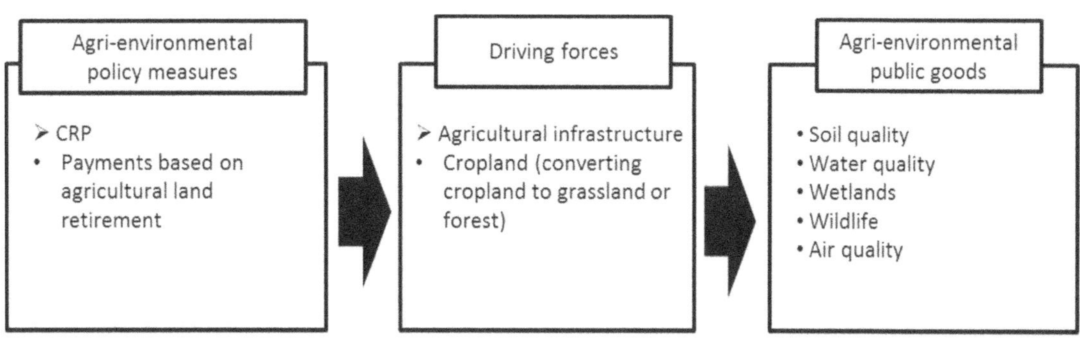

CRP: Conservation Reserve Program.

Input-based instruments, output-based instruments and multiple objectives

The discussion on multiple objectives and targeting is related to that on input-based instruments and output-based instruments. Currently, most agri-environmental policy measures are input-based that target multiple agri-environmental public goods.

The main purpose of policy measures is to address market failure associated with agriculture. In other words, to provide the adequate amount of agri-environmental public goods is the purpose of the policy measures. However, the four patterns of policy measures examined do not directly target agri-environmental public goods. As a result, it is not always clear to what extent policy measures can address the market failure and to what extent they can effectively increase the supply of agri-environmental public goods to the point where demand meets supply. Examining the relationship between driving forces (inputs) and agri-environmental public goods (outcomes) is important to overcome market failure by government intervention.

In some cases, more careful design of input-based policy instruments is necessary. For instance, many agri-environmental payments are paid if farmers adopt various good farming practices. Farmers can choose what practices they adopt, depending on their situations, and try to maximise their private profits when taking into consideration the agri-environmental programmes. Because an increasing number of good farming practices are being adopted, it can be assumed that the amount of agri-environmental public goods provided are also increasing. However, due to the multiple effects that each farming practice has on agri-environmental public goods, they may not in fact be increasing as intended by policy makers. Farmers may choose farming practices that can be easily adopted, but which are not necessarily those that have the largest environmental effects. Depending on the targeted agri-environmental public goods, policy makers may need to limit the number of good farming practices from which farmers can choose, or target outputs rather than inputs. Depending on the number of targeted agri-environmental public goods, best farming practices may also differ. If an input-based policy measure targets a specific agri-environmental public good, the farming practice adopted should be useful in providing that good, while if an input-based policy measure targets multiple agri-environmental public goods, the farming practice adopted should be decided based on its potential total impacts on the environment. Moreover, when private and public benefits differ, farmers may not be providing agri-environmental public goods that the public demands, even if farmers are adopting farming practices.

In addition, considering the fact that a driving force affects multiple agri-environmental public goods, output-based policy measures may also need to target not only one agri-environmental public goods, but also multiple agri-environmental public goods. For instance, assuming there is an output-based payment for improving water quality. Farmers choose their best farming practices to improve water quality to apply for and receive the payment. But, these farming practices may bring other benefits such as biodiversity or soil protection and quality. If this is the case, even if water quality improved by the adopted farming practices itself is not enough to qualify for the application criteria of the output-based payment, the combined environmental performance (improved water quality and biodiversity as well as soil protection and quality) may be able to surpass a certain point and bring larger environmental benefits. Therefore, performance-based payments may also need to consider multiple effects of agri-environmental public goods, not just one agri-environmental public good.

Considering the fact that many policy measures address multiple objectives, setting appropriate environmental targets for agri-environmental public goods is challenging. Recently, in the United Kingdom, an environmental account project tries to calculate overall environmental impacts (both positive and negative) associated with agriculture (Box 5.4). If it is possible to understand how policy measures can improve multiple environmental objectives by using this environmental account, this approach may be able to shift agri-environmental policy measures more to the evidence-based and performance-based measures.

Box 5.4. Environmental Accounts for Agriculture in the United Kingdom

The United Kingdom Department for Environment Food and Rural Affaires (Defra) calculated Environmental Accounts for Agriculture (Jones et al., 2015; McVittie et al., 2009; RISE, 2009). Figure 5.6 shows the result. This shows three trends: total benefits from agriculture, total damages from agriculture and total benefits less damages. The main benefits come from biodiversity and landscape, while the main damages relate to greenhouse gas emissions, air quality and water quality (Jones et al., 2015; RISE, 2009). Currently, the total damages outweigh the total benefits. Thus, improving the overall environment associated with agriculture is a key policy challenge in the United Kingdom.

Figure 5.6. Environmental accounts for agriculture in the United Kingdom

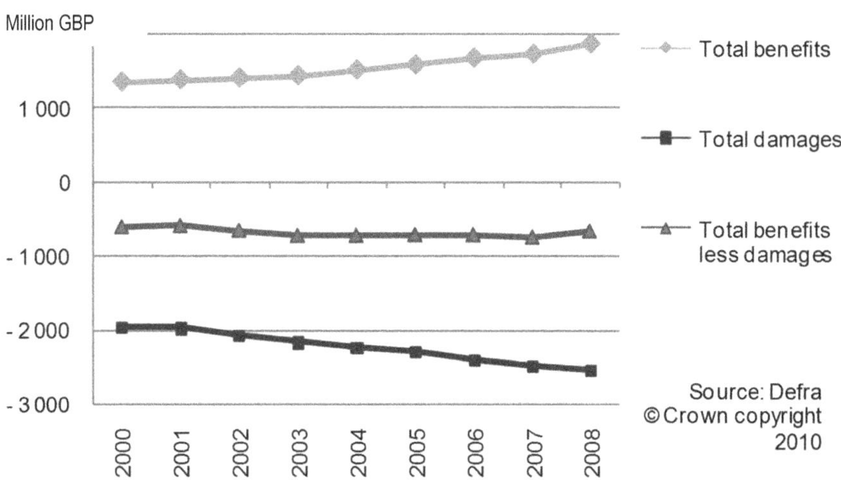

Source: Defra (2010), *Agricultural Change and Environment Observatory Programme*: graph based on data derived from Jacobs and SA (2008), *Environmental Accounts for Agriculture*.

Agri-environmental policies and policy mixes

A single policy measure often targets multiple agri-environmental public goods. And also, multiple policy measures are usually implemented for a single agri-environmental public good. Table 5.4 summarises the policy measures implemented for each agri-environmental public good in the OECD case study countries, and it shows effective policy mixes are a key to improving the cost-effectiveness of policy measures and achieving environmental targets.

Regulatory requirements are used in many of the countries studied, in particular for soil protection and quality, water quality and quantity, air quality, and biodiversity; this is not the case, however for climate change and resilience to natural disasters. In many cases, regulatory requirements cover not only farmers, but also non-famers and non-agricultural sectors. They typically establish mandatory environmental quality levels that society tries to maintain.

Environmental taxes and charges are used in the Netherlands for water quantity and agricultural landscapes. Environmental taxes seek to alter the economic incentives of farmers and to correct incentive failures due to missing markets for agri-environmental public goods; price incentives are replaced with administered taxes or charges (OECD, 2010a).

Agri-environmental payments are the main policy instruments for most agri-environmental public goods in the case study countries. Those based on farming practices (input-based instruments) are used the most, and those based on outcomes are limited and used only in the United States. Even there, payments are not based on actual environmental outcomes but instead the Conservation Stewardship Program (CSP) uses a points system to determine conservation performance. The rankings established become the basis upon which applicants are selected and payments determined. The CSP is used for addressing various agri-environmental public goods such as soil protection and quality, water quality and quantity, air quality and biodiversity.

Tradable rights and permits are used, but are still limited to specific cases. Australia relies exclusively on water rights to control water quantity, while other countries implement multiple policy measures for managing water quantity.

Community-based measures are used in Australia, the Netherlands and Japan for some local agri-environmental public goods such as soil quality, water quality and quantity, and biodiversity. Collective action can involve local communities and local groups (local people, local NGOs, local authorities, etc.) and leverage resources among members, and cover broader areas that are necessary for providing agri-environmental public goods (OECD, 2013).

Lastly, facilitative measures such as technical assistance and extension are used widely for many agri-environmental public goods in the all case study countries. These measures are particularly useful when farmers are unaware of the importance of potential agri-environmental public goods. Typically, these facilitative measures are used with other policy measures, such as payments and regulations.

Effective policy mixes are key to enhancing the cost-effectiveness of policy measures and achieving environmental targets. Among the nine agri-environmental public goods targeted in the case study countries, all countries use a mix of policy measures for biodiversity (the total number of policy measures (X) in Table 5.4 is 29; the average is 5.8 per country). This large number reflects the complexity of biodiversity issues. Policy mixes are also used for other agri-environmental public goods such as water quality (total 23: average 4.6) and water quantity (total 21: average 4.2), followed by soil protection and quality (total 19: average 3.8), and air quality (total 15: average 3). In the two European countries (the United Kingdom and the Netherlands), many policy measures are mixed where agricultural landscapes are concerned (a total of 13 for an average of 7.5), but there are few policy measures that address agricultural landscapes in Japan and the United States (a total of 4 for an average of 2).

Box 5.5 provides an example of policy mixes for addressing an agri-environmental public good in the United States.

Table 5.4. Agri-environmental policy measures and targeted agri-environmental public goods in the studied OECD countries

		Soil protection and quality					Water quality					Water quantity/availability				
		AUS	GBR	NLD	JPN	USA	AUS	GBR	NLD	JPN	USA	AUS	GBR	NLD	JPN	USA
Regulatory	Regulatory requirements	X		X	X		X	X	X	X	X		X	X	X	X
	Environmental taxes/ charges													X		
	Environmental cross-compliance		X	X		X		X	X				X	X		
Financial incentives	Payments based on farming practices	X	X		X	X	X	X			X			X	X	X
	Payments based on land retirement					X		X			X			X		X
	Payments based on farm fixed assets		X		X			X		X			X			
	Payments based on outcomes					X					X					X
	Tradable rights/permits										X	X	X			X
	Community based measures	X					X			X					X	
Facilitative	Technical assistance/ extension/ R&D/ labelling/standards/certification	X	X		X	X	X	X		X	X		X			X
		Air quality					Climate change (greenhouse gas emissions)					Climate change (carbon storage)				
		AUS	GBR	NLD	JPN	USA	AUS	GBR	NLD	JPN	USA	AUS	GBR	NLD	JPN	USA
Regulatory	Regulatory requirements	X	X	X	X	X		X								
	Environmental taxes/charges															
	Environmental cross-compliance			X											X	
Financial incentives	Payments based on farming practices		X			X	X	X				X	X		X	
	Payments based on land retirement					X							X			
	Payments based on farm fixed assets			X	X			X	X					X		
	Payments based on outcomes					X										
	Tradable rights/permits								X	X						
	Community based measures								X					X		
Facilitative	Technical assistance/ extension/R&D/ labelling/standards/certification			X	X	X		X	X	X			X	X		

continued

Table 5.4. Agri-environmental policy measures and targeted agri-environmental public goods in the studied OECD countries (*cont.*)

		Biodiversity					Agricultural landscapes					Resilience to natural disaster				
		AUS	GBR	NLD	JPN	USA	AUS	GBR	NLD	JPN	USA	AUS	GBR	NLD	JPN	USA
Regulatory	Regulatory requirements	X	X	X		X			X		X					
	Environmental taxes/charges								X							
	Environmental cross-compliance		X	X	X	X		X	X		X		X	X		
Financial incentives	Payments based on farming practices	X	X	X	X	X		X	X	X			X		X	
	Payments based on land retirement		X	X		X		X	X				X			
	Payments based on farm fixed assets			X				X								
	Payments based on outcomes					X										
	Tradable rights/permits	X		X		X			X							
	Community based measures	X		X	X				X	X					X	
Facilitative	Technical assistance/ extension/R&D/ labelling/standards/certification	X	X	X	X	X		X	X		X		X	X		

1. As explained in Chapter 1, these targeted goods are not always public goods. Sometimes, they can be private goods (e.g. agricultural landscape with use value by visitors can be a private good if exclusion can be made) or when they cause harm, they can be defined as private bads or public bads (Kolstad, 2011). Careful examination on whether these goods have characteristics of non-rivalry and/or non-excludability is necessary for each case.
2. This table is not meant to convey the policy measures used most frequently in each country.
3. For the details of the policy programmes, see Annex Table A1-A5 and country case studies (Jones et al., 2015; Pannell and Roberts, 2015; Schrijver and Uetake, 2015; Shortle and Uetake, 2015; Uetake, 2015).

Box 5.5. An examples of policy mixes: Water quality in the United States

Water quality is a major agri-environmental public good targeted in the United States. To improve water quality, a set of policy instruments are implemented by the federal and state governments, including regulatory requirements, payments based on farming practices and technical assistance, tradable credits and environmental taxes. Regulatory measures mainly address agricultural point sources while the others target agricultural nonpoint sources. Both approaches are necessary for improving water quality in the United States.

Regulatory measures (agricultural point sources)

The Clean Water Act (CWA) was enacted in 1972 to respond to the highly degraded state of surface water quality. The principle mechanism for water quality protection under the CWA is the National Pollutant Discharge Elimination System (NPDES) which requires point sources of water pollution to obtain NPDES discharge permits in order to be allowed to discharge pollutants. While the NPDES mechanism mainly regulate industrial and municipal dischargers, large Concentrated Animal Feeding Operations (CAFO) also need to get NPDES permits for discharging pollutants into stream. While CAFOs can be significant local sources of surface water pollutants, most agricultural pollution loads are nonpoint sources. As a result, the NPDES mechanism is largely inapplicable to agriculture.

Payments and technical assistance (agricultural nonpoint sources)

To address non-point source pollutions by agriculture, both state and federal governments encourage the adoption of agricultural pollution control practices (Best management Practices or BMPs) through education, technical assistance, and financial support through cost-sharing subsidies.

Currently, the United States Department of Agriculture (USDA) administers several programmes that provide farmers with financial assistance to adopt BMPs. The largest programme is the Environmental Quality Incentives Program (EQIP) with current annual funding of USD 1.3 billion. Other USDA programmes that can have positive water quality impacts include the Conservation Reserve Program (CRP) and the Conservation Stewardship Program (CSP).

Tradable credits (agricultural nonpoint sources)

In addition, some states (e.g. Pennsylvania and Ohio) have developed pollution trading programmes that enable industrial and municipal polluters to meet their NPDES permit requirements through the purchase of pollution reduction credits from agriculture. Most of these trading programmes address nutrients.

Environmental taxes (agricultural nonpoint sources)

Florida uses an innovative incentive, "agricultural privilege tax", imposed on cropland to fund pollution control initiatives in the Everglades Agricultural Area. Farmers can get collective credits (i.e. reductions in the tax rate) against the privilege tax if they reduce phosphorus discharges below a 25% reduction goal for the basin. The programme also provides individual farmers with credits based on farm-specific performance.

Source: Shortle and Uetake (2015), "Public Goods and Externalities: Agri-environmental Policy Measures in the United States".

Synergies or conflicts

There are many good reasons for applying a mix of instruments to provide agri-environmental public goods, rather than relying on a single one. This is because a majority of agri-environmental public goods have "multiple aspects". For example, water quality issues associated with nutrients has to be considered from the aspects of the total amount of surplus nutrients in an area as well as when, where and how nutrients are applied to the fields, etc. Policy impacts on a single agri-environmental public good often affects other such goods as well, and this must be taken into consideration (de Groot et al., 2010; Helin et al., 2013). In general, it is best to apply agri-environmental policy instruments as close to the underlying agri-environmental public goods as possible. However, in several cases it is difficult to apply instruments that target the agri-environmental public goods directly. For instance, it is not practical to measure the run-off of nutrients from individual farms to surface or groundwater. In such situations, one or more "proxy instruments" may need to be applied (OECD, 2007c). Like the United States (Box 5.5), one possible approach is to apply regulatory measures to agricultural point sources (e.g. large livestock farm) at the same time that financial incentives (e.g. payments, tradable credits) are applied to agricultural nonpoint sources.

In some cases, policy mixes are implemented usefully, while in others some instruments have negative impacts on either the environmental effectiveness or the economic efficiency of the overall instrument mix or both. There may be situations where the environmental effectiveness or the economic efficiency of an instrument mix is jeopardised because some potential instruments are not applied or are only very partially applied. The consequences of unaligned policies can be serious (OECD, 2007c). Moreover, sometimes, some farming practices can bring both positive and negative impacts on the environment (ENRD, 2010). For instance, in the Netherlands, higher water tables in peat areas can reduce carbon emissions. However, this higher water tables cause higher methane and nitrous oxide emissions (Schrijver and Uetake, 2015). If policy measures just try to target higher water tables, there is a risk of net environmental damage. Therefore, other policy measures targeting methane and nitrous oxide emissions are also necessary.

A recent OECD study on climate change, water and agriculture also revealed that climate change mitigation practices may have positive or negative implications on agricultural water management and on water quality. The potential synergies and trade-offs between mitigation and agricultural management practices are site-specific and for many cases there are substantial knowledge gaps. It is important to recognise these linkages in the design of mitigation policies, to reduce the risk of conflict between mitigation and water policy objectives, and to maximise potential synergies (OECD, 2014). Coordination mechanisms to overcome conflicts between environmental goals are needed.

In particular, agri-environmental policies are designed and developed by various government departments, both at national and local levels. For instance, in the United States, at the Federal level, the United States Department of Agriculture (USDA), United States Environmental Protection Agency (USEPA), United States Fish and Wildlife Service and United States Army Corps of Engineers develop programmes. State governments also develop various programmes, sometimes mandated by federal law, and other times at their own initiative (Table 5.5) (Shortle and Uetake, 2015). This highlights the importance of co-ordination within agricultural ministries, and between agricultural ministries and other ministries such as environmental ministries and local governments.

Table 5.5. Multiple agencies related to agri-environmental policies (the case of the United States)

Federal government	
Provides the "supreme law of the land" on agri-environmental public goods where Congress legislates within its constitutionally authorised powers	
US Department of Agriculture	Primary federal agency for provision of agri-environmental public goods of all types.
US Environmental Protection Agency	Primary federal agency for pesticide regulation (Federal Insecticide, Fungicide, and Rodenticide Act), and for enforcing federal air and water pollution control laws (Clean Air Act, Clean Water Act, Coastal Zone Act, Reauthorization Amendments). Agriculture is largely exempted from direct federal air and water quality regulation.
US Fish and Wildlife Service	Authorities related to endangered species protection (Endangered Species Act).
US Army Corps of Engineers	Authorities related to wetlands protection (Clean Water Act).
State and local governments	
(1) Authorities delegated to state, local, and sometimes tribal governments by the federal government in areas where federal law is supreme (e.g. The Clean Air and Clean Water Acts delegate significant water pollution control authorities relevant to agriculture to the states);	
(2) State and local agri-environmental policy initiatives (sometimes undertake collaboratively with the federal government) in areas that are not contradictory to federal law in regulatory domains covered by federal law (e.g. State and local agencies work collaboratively with federal agencies to implement USDA and other federal agri-environmental laws and programmes);	
(3) States and local initiatives in areas that have not been pre-empted by federal legislation (e.g. State and local agencies are the primary actors for protecting agricultural landscapes).	

Source: Adapted from Shortle and Uetake (2015), *Public Goods and Externalities: Agri-environmental Policy Measures in the United States*, OECD Publishing, Paris.

Policy measures have been developed to address various agri-environmental issues and the backgrounds of introducing these policy measures are different one by one. Moreover, various government sections are involved in policy designs. As a result, in many cases, current agri-environmental policy measures are very complex. For example, to address biodiversity issues, a number of policy measures are implemented in the studied OECD countries simultaneously. In order to understand the current situation of policy measures, at both national and local levels, and examine whether these policy measures have synergies or conflicts, developing a policy matrix table (Annex Table A1-5) is useful. Beyond the boundaries of departments and institutions, it is important to design appropriate policy mixes for providing agri-environmental public goods.

Policy mixes and additionality

A complex set of policy measures questions the *additionality* of a policy measure. Additionality refers to whether the environmental services associated with agriculture that are supported under a given programme would have been provided in the absence of the programme (Mezzatesta et al., 2013). A policy measure has full additionality if all participating farmers needed the incentive provided by the scheme to change their farming practices or improve their environmental performance, and would not have done so in the absence of the scheme. On the other hand, additionality is low when a large proportion of incentive recipients would have changed their behaviour or complied with the programme requirements even without the incentive (OECD, 2012a). In the context of policy mixes, this is particularly important because some policies can be redundant and may not be able to bring high additionality, if policy mixes are not well developed.

A recent OECD study on environmental co-benefits and stacking (a single agri-environmental practice produces several environmental outputs and earns credits from multiple environmental markets) in environmental markets (Lankoski et al., 2015) examines environmental credit markets and offset schemes related to ecosystem services (carbon sequestration and water quality). By undertaking a numerical simulation of the Corn Belt in the United States, it shows that allowing stacking has a possibility to bring additionality through increased participation of farmers in a programme and through increased adoption of environmental practices.

Some countries also try to examine the additionality of their country programmes. For example, OECD (2012c) studied the additionality of agri-environmental payments targeting the adoption of conservation practices in the United States and, based on the Agricultural Resources Management Survey 2009 and 2010, he identified that among the wheat and corn producers surveyed a considerable number of them adopted the targeted conservation practices without the stimulus of an incentive payment, either because they are profitable on their farms (conservation tillage) or because targeted practices are required by state regulations (nutrient or manure management). Mezzatesta et al. (2013) analysed cost-shared programmes to promote conservation practices in Ohio in the United States, and found that the degree of additionality among conservation practices varied depending on practices: high additionality for hayfield establishments, cover crops and filter stripes, while low additionality for conservation tillage. Additionality of agri-environmental schemes in the United Kingdom was found for agricultural landscapes and biodiversity in Environmentally Sensitive Areas (Boatman et al., 2008). Boatman et al. recommended that short- and long-term monitoring and evaluation, incorporating baseline data and repeat surveys for key indicators, should be implemented for agri-environmental schemes to ensure that they could bring additionality.

Policy mixes of payments may bring larger environmental effects if additionality is considered. For example, Busch (2013) found that a mixture of carbon payments and biodiversity payments has the potential to provide greater incentives than would an equal amount of money spent only on carbon payments if payments are allocated more towards new suppliers (high additionality) than to existing suppliers (low additionality). However, policies that focus on additionality may raise a concern on equity, since these programmes give a lower (or no) payment to farmers who have voluntarily adopted improved practices; these farmers would consider themselves penalised compared to others (OECD, 2010a).

Evaluating the effects of additionality is challenging due to the lack of data and the complexity of agri-environmental programmes. To identify whether gains are additional or not, estimation of a baseline is necessary (Claassen et al., 2008). Identifying the extent to which farmers can voluntarily provide agri-environmental public goods without government intervention is necessary to avoid paying farmers who would have improved their environmental performance without a payment, and develop better policy mixes.

Farmer behaviour and policy mixes

When designing good agri-environmental policy mixes, it is important to understand farmer behaviour. Various factors, including external (financial and effort benefits/costs), internal (habits and cognitive processes), and social (societal norms and cultural attitudes), affect farmer behaviour (OECD, 2012b, 2013).

Financial incentives are clearly important because new farming practices will not be adopted if they are not profitable. Financial incentives alone, however, cannot explain all changes in farmer behaviour because these affect only external factors (OECD, 2012b; Van Herzele et al., 2013). To provide agri-environmental public goods, a holistic approach that combines market-based instruments and other tools which can influence farmer behaviour in terms of habits, cognition and norms is necessary. "Nudging," a small change in the social context that alters behaviour without forcing anyone to do anything, is a one way to affect internal and social factors. For example, "visualisation" policies such as labelling (carbon foot-printing) can encourage farmers to establish what they need to do, while their efforts can be conveyed to consumers through labelling. Consequently, identifying and labelling farmers as "ecologically co-operative" is a visible method that could complement financial incentive measures to address various related agri-environmental public goods (OECD, 2012b).

Policy choices

Best policy measures for agri-environmental public goods which can apply to all kinds of situations do not exist. A case-by-case analysis will inevitably have to be made (Claassen et al., 2001; OECD, 2007c). However, as a general rule, an optimally chosen instrument would equate the marginal social benefits and marginal social costs. Estimating benefits to society in the absence of well-functioning markets is of course a major difficulty. As a result, most agri-environmental policy measures concentrate on the costs of provision which are usually easier to assess (OECD, 2008). If multiple payments exist, it is necessary to pay attention to potential overlap of these payments, and promote good farming practices in a cost-effective way by targeting marginal changes as much as possible.

One simple basic approach for policy mixes and policy choices identified in this book is to use the reference level framework (Chapter 4). Farmers are obliged to meet the minimum level of environmental quality at their own expense. Thus, environmental regulations may be needed. But, beyond the reference level to reach environmental targets, agri-environmental payments may be necessary to promote environmentally friendly farming. Technical assistance can support these activities and through the combination of financial incentives, it would be able to address heterogeneous farmer behaviour as well. For instance, to improve water quality, many countries set water quality regulations and farmers have to reduce nitrates from agricultural sources. To further improve water quality, payments to farmers who adopt good management practices and/or technical assistance are provided. Reference levels and environmental targets are not always clearly defined and policy mixes and choices by using the framework of reference levels is still limited in many OECD countries.

Pannell (2008) also discusses the choice of policy instruments for encouraging environmentally beneficial land-use change. His analysis suggests that instrument choice should depend on the relative levels of private (or internal) and public (or external) net benefits (Box 5.6).

Box 5.6. Framework of policy choices

Pannell (2008) outlines what policy mechanism, if any, policy makers should choose in order to maximise the net benefits of intervention (Figure 5.7 presents a summary of his analysis). According to Pannell, *private net benefits* are defined as the benefits minus costs accruing to the private land manager as a result of proposed changes in land management, whereas *public net benefits* are benefits minus costs accruing to everyone other than the private land manager. In this way, the private net benefit dimension provides insight into the behaviour of the landholder, while the public net benefit dimension relates to the effects on everyone else that flow from the landholder's behaviour. The latter effects, commonly referred to as *externalities*, can be used as justification by governments taking action to try to influence the behaviour of economic agents, when they are non-excludable (the nature of the good is such that it is impossible to exclude anyone from consuming it) and non-rival (the same good can be consumed by anyone without diminishing the consumption opportunities available to others). Projects with positive *public* net benefits fall in the top half of the figure, while projects with positive *private* net benefits fall in the right half of the figure.

Figure 5.7. Efficient policy mechanisms based on a simple set of rules

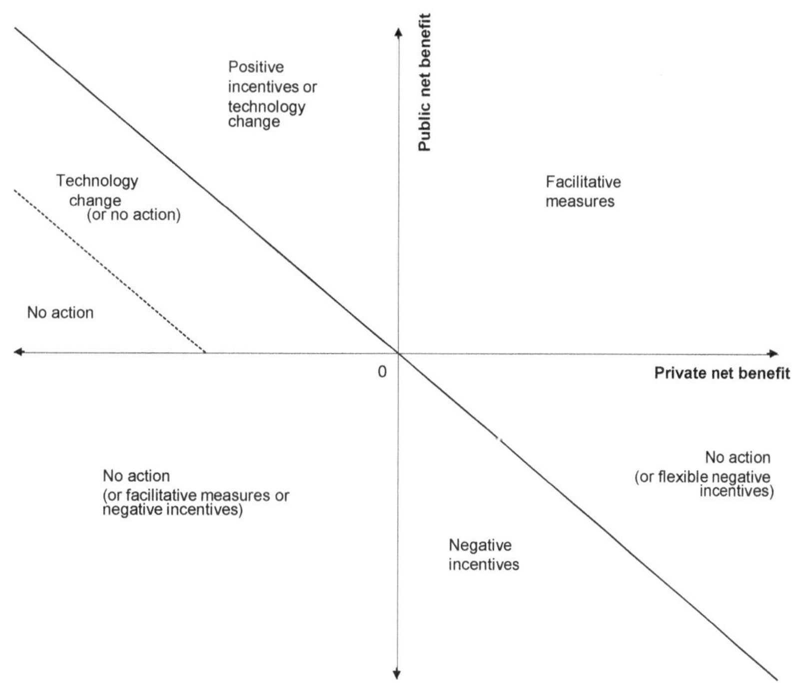

Source: Adopted from Pannell, D. J. (2008), "Public Benefits, Private Benefits, and Policy Intervention for Land-use Change for Environmental Benefits", *Land Economics*, Vol. 84, No. 2, pp. 225-240.

Based on the framework, he suggests using the following policy mechanisms as follows:

- ***Positive incentives*** where public net benefits are highly positive and negative private net benefits are close to zero.
- ***Negative incentives*** where negative public net benefits clearly outweigh slightly positive private net benefits.
- ***Facilitative measures*** (extension services to farmers) where public net benefits are highly positive and private net benefits are slightly positive.
- ***Technology development*** where negative private net benefits outweigh or are similar to public net benefits.
- ***No action*** where private net benefits outweigh negative public net benefits, or if public net benefits and private net *benefits* are both negative, and thus in both cases the land-use change should be accepted.

It is notable that the areas for positive and negative incentives and facilitative measures are only the sub-sets of the total. According to Pannell (2008) this framework reveals that the selection of cost-effective measures may be more sensitive to private net benefits than to public net benefits. Moreover, policy measures, such as positive and negative incentives and facilitative measures, are more likely to generate high pay-offs if the private net benefits are close to zero. This is because land-use change can be prompted (prevented) with small positive (negative) incentives.

In many cases, multiple objectives are targeted by multiple policy measures and it is not always clear to what extent a particular policy measure tries to address the issue, and to what extent other policy measures do so. Their reference levels are not clear enough either. Each policy's target, reference levels and the relations with other policy measures should be carefully reviewed.

For good agri-environmental policy mixes and choices, careful assessments of any new instruments and regular *ex ante* and *ex post* assessments of all instruments impacting on agri-environmental public goods are necessary. In order to develop instrument mixes that are environmentally effective and economically efficient, it is important to enhance possibilities for instruments to mutually reinforce each other by applying instruments that provide flexibility, and pay attention to the incentive impacts of various instrument-design options. It is necessary to avoid overlapping instruments, except when they can mutually reinforce each other, or address different aspects of the environmental problem. Appropriate monitoring and enforcement mechanisms are essential (OECD, 2007c).

Equity and social factors

Policy makers also take social factors such as income distribution and equity between and among different groups (producers, consumers, and taxpayers) into consideration in order to develop policy choices. It can be the case that more than one type of instrument will be capable of producing a cost-effective outcome, but each will yield different distributions of wealth and will therefore be viewed differently from an equity perspective (OECD, 2010a).

In some cases, targeting community-based activities can include all farmers and local people who concern their local environmental issues without excluding them and may be able to ease the concern on equity. The policy design of agri-environmental policies requires the consideration of environmental, economic and social factors as well as practical constraints such as administrative costs.

Notes

1. For details of each policy measure in the selected OECD countries, please refer to the country case studies.
2. The European Union launched a CLIAM project that aims to produce the knowledge base to support an effective CAP policy design in the direction of improved landscape management. For more information, see www.claimproject.eu/index.aspx.

References

Bamière, L., M. David and B. Vermont (2013), "Agri-environmental Policies for Biodiversity When the Spatial Pattern of the Reserve Matters", *Ecological Economics*, Vol. 85, pp. 97-104.

Barreiro-Hurlé, J., M. Espinosa-Goded and P. Dupraz (2010), "Does Intensity of Change Matter? Factors Affecting Adoption of Agrienvironmental Schemes in Spain," *Journal of Environmental Planning and Management* Vol. 53, No. 7, pp. 891–905.

Boatman, N., et al. (2008), *A Review of Environmental Benefits Supplied by Agri-environment Schemes*. FST20/79/041, Report to the Land Use Policy Group, United Kingdom.

Busch, J. (2013), "Supplementing REDD+ with Biodiversity Payment: The Paradox of Paying for Multiple Ecosystem Services," *Land Economics*, Vol. 89, No. 4, pp. 655-675, http://le.uwpress.org/content/89/4/655.refs.

Claassen, R. A. Cattaneo and R. Johansson (2008), "Cost-effective Design of Agri-environmental Payment Programs: U.S. Experience in Theory and Practice," *Ecological Economics*, Vol. 65, pp. 737-752.

Claassen, R. et al. (2001), "Agri-environmental Policy at the Crossroads: Guideposts on a Changing Landscape", *Agricultural Economic Report*, Number 794, Economic Research Service/USDA, Washington, D.C.

Cong, R.G. et al. (2014), "Managing Ecosystem Services for Agriculture: Will Landscape-scale Management Pay?," *Ecological Economics*, Vol. 99, pp. 53-62.

Defra (2010), *Agricultural Change and Environment Observatory Programme*, Defra. London. http://archive.defra.gov.uk/evidence/economics/foodfarm/reports/envacc/ (accessed 6 September 2013).

Dunn, H. (2011), "Payments for Ecosystem Services", *Defra Evidence and Analysis Series, Paper 4*, Defra, London.

European Network for Rural Development (ENRD) (2010), *Thematic Working Group 3: Public goods and Public Intervention: Final Report*, ENRD, Brussels.

Goldman, R.L., B.H. Thompson and G.C. Daily (2007), "Institutional Incentives for Managing the Landscape: Inducing Cooperation for the Production of Ecosystem Services," *Ecological Economics*, Vol. 64, pp. 333-343.

de Groot, R.S. et al. (2010), "Challenges in Integrating the Concept of Ecosystem Services and Values in Landscape Planning, Management and Decision Making," *Ecological Complexity*, Vol. 7, pp. 260-272.

Helin, J., et al. (2013), "Model for Quantifying the Synergies between Farmland Biodiversity Conservation and Water Protection at Catchment Scale," *Journal of Environmental Management*, Vol. 131, pp. 307-317.

Jacobs and SAC (2008), *Environmental Accounts for Agriculture,* Defra, London.

Jones, J., P. Silcock and T. Uetake (2015), "Public Goods and Externalities: Agri-environmental Policy Measures in the United Kingdom", *OECD Food, Agriculture and Fisheries Papers*, No. 83, OECD Publishing, Paris.
DOI: http://dx.doi.org/10.1787/5js08hw4drd1-en.

Kolstad, C.D. (2011), *Intermediate Environmental Economics: International Second Edition*, Oxford University Press, New York.

Lankoski, J., et al. (2015), "Environmental Co-benefits and Stacking in Environmental Markets", *OECD Food, Agriculture and Fisheries Papers*, No. 72, OECD Publishing, Paris. DOI: http://dx.doi.org/10.1787/5js6g5khdvhj-en.

Madureira, L. et al. (2013), *Feasibility Study on the Valuation of Public Goods and Externalities in EU Agriculture: Final Report*, A Study Commissioned by European Commission Joint Research Centre, Institute for Prospective Technological Studies Agriculture and life Sciences in the Economy, Contract No. 152423. University of Trás-os-Montes e Alto Douro.

McVittie, A., D. Moran and S. Thomson (2009), *A Review of Literature on the Value of Public goods from Agriculture and the Production Impacts of the Single Farm Payment Scheme*, Rural Policy Centre Research Report, Report Prepared for the Scottish Government's Rural and Environment Research and Analysis Directorate (RERAD/004/09), SAC, Edinburgh.

Mezzatesta, B., D.A. Newburn and R.T. Woodward (2013), "Additionality and the Adoption of Farm Conservation Practices," *Land Economics*, Vol. 89. No. 4, pp. 722-742.

OECD (2014), *Climate Change, Water and Agriculture: Towards Resilient Systems*, OECD Studies on Water, OECD Publishing, Paris. DOI: http://dx.doi.org/10.1787/9789264209138-en.

OECD (2013), *Providing Agri-environmental Public Goods through Collective Action*, OECD Publishing, Paris. DOI: http://dx.doi.org/10.1787/9789264197213-en.

OECD (2012a), *Evaluation of Agri-environmental Policies: Selected Methodological Issues and Case Studies*, OECD Publishing, Paris. doi: 10.1787/9789264179332-en.

OECD (2012b), *Farmer Behaviour, Agricultural Management and Climate Change*, OECD Publishing, Paris. doi: 10.1787/9789264167650-en.

OECD (2012c), "Additionality in US agri-environmental programmes for working land: A preliminary look at new data", in OECD, *Evaluation of Agri-environmental Policies: Selected Methodological Issues and Case Studies*, OECD Publishing, Paris. DOI: http://dx.doi.org/10.1787/9789264179332-7-en

OECD (2011), *A Green Growth Strategy for Food and Agriculture Preliminary Report*, OECD, Paris, http://www.oecd.org/greengrowth/sustainable-agriculture/48224529.pdf.

OECD (2010a), *Guidelines for Cost-effective Agri-environmental Policy Measures*, OECD Publishing, Paris. DOI: http://dx.doi.org/10.1787/9789264086845-en.

OECD (2010b), *Environmental Cross Compliance in Agriculture*, OECD, Paris, http://www.oecd.org/tad/sustainable-agriculture/44737935.pdf.

OECD (2008), "Agricultural Policy Design and Implementation: A Synthesis", *OECD Food, Agriculture and Fisheries Papers*, No. 7, OECD Publishing, Paris. DOI: http://dx.doi.org/10.1787/243786286663.

OECD (2007a), *Effective Targeting of Agricultural Policies: Best Practices for Policy Design and Implementation*, OECD Publishing, Paris. DOI: http://dx.doi.org/10.1787/9789264038288-en.

OECD (2007b), *The Implementation Costs of Agricultural Policies*, OECD Publishing, Paris. DOI: http://dx.doi.org/10.1787/9789264024540-en..

OECD (2007c), *Instrument Mixes for Environmental Policy*, OECD Publishing, Paris. DOI: http://dx.doi.org/10.1787/9789264018419-en.

OECD (2006), "Financing Agricultural Policies with Particular Reference to Public Good Provision and Multifunctionality: Which Level Of Government?", [AGR/CA/APM(2005)19/FINAL], Paris.

OECD (2001), *Improving the Environmental Performance of Agriculture: Policy options and market approaches*, OECD Publishing, Paris. DOI: http://dx.doi.org/10.1787/9789264033801-en.

Pannell, D. (2008), "Public Benefits, Private Benefits, and Policy Intervention for Land-use Change for Environmental Benefits", *Land Economics*, Vol. 84, No. 2, pp. 225-240, https://muse.jhu.edu/login?auth=0&type=summary&url=/journals/land_economics/v084/84.2.pannell.pdf.

Pannell, D. and A. Roberts (2015), "Public goods and externalities: agri-environmental policy measures in Australia", *OECD Food, Agriculture and Fisheries Papers*, No. 80, OECD Publishing, Paris. DOI: http://dx.doi.org/10.1787/5js08hx1btlw-en.

Ribaudo, M. (2013), *Policy Instruments for Protecting Environmental Quality.* www.ers.usda.gov/topics/natural-resources-environment/environmental-quality/policy-instruments-for-protecting-environmental-quality.aspx#.Uh4f_j_leq0 . Accessed 18 September 2013.

Ribaudo, M., L. Hansen, D. Hellerstein and C. Greene (2008), "The Use of Markets to Increase Private Investment in Environmental Stewardship", United States Department of Agriculture, Economic Research Service, *Economic Research Report* Number 64, Washington D.C.

RISE (2009), *RISE Task Force on Public Goods from Private Land*, Directed by A. Buckwell, RISE (Rural Investment Support Europe).

Sakuyama, T. (2005), *Incentive Measures for Environmental Services from Agriculture: Briefing Note on the Roles of Agriculture Project in the FAO: Socio-economic Analysis and Policy Implications of the Roles of Agriculture in Developing Countries*, Food and Agriculture Organization Publications, Rome.

Schrijver, R. and T. Uetake (2015), "Public goods and externalities: agri-environmental policy measures in the Netherlands", *OECD Food, Agriculture and Fisheries Papers*, No. 82, OECD Publishing, Paris. DOI: http://dx.doi.org/10.1787/5js08hwpr1q8-en.

Shortle, J. and T. Uetake (2015), "Public Goods and Externalities: Agri-environmental Policy Measures in the the United States", *OECD Food, Agriculture and Fisheries Papers*, No. 84, OECD Publishing, Paris. DOI: http://dx.doi.org/10.1787/5js08hwhg8mw-en.

Uetake, T. (2015), "Public goods and externalities: agri-environmental policy measures in Japan", *OECD Food, Agriculture and Fisheries Papers*, No. 81, OECD Publishing, Paris. DOI: http://dx.doi.org/10.1787/5js08hwsjj26-en.

Uetake T. and H. Sasaki (2014), "Promoting Agri-environmental Policies to Meet the Consumer Preference in Japan: Economic-Biophysical Model Approach", Paper presented at the 139th EAAE (European Association of Agricultural Economics) Seminar, 17-21 February 2014, Innsbruk-lgls, Austria.

Van Herzele, A. et al. (2013), "Effort for Money? Farmers' Rationale for Participation in Agri-environment Measures with Different Implementation Complexity," *Journal of Environmental Management*, Vol. 131, pp. 110-120.

Vojtech, V. (2010), "Policy Measures Addressing Agri-environmental Issues", *OECD Food, Agriculture and Fisheries Papers*, No. 24, OECD Publishing, Paris. DOI: http://dx.doi.org/10.1787/5kmjrzg08vvb-en.

Chapter 6

Policy implications for the provision of agri-environmental goods

This chapter presents the conclusions and policy implications of agri-environmental measures in the selected OECD countries of this study: Australia, Japan, the Netherlands, the United Kingdom and the United States.

Public goods and externalities in the agri-environmental sector

Agriculture is a provider of commodities such as food, feed, fibre and fuel and, it can also bring both positive and negative impacts on the environment such as biodiversity, water and soil quality. These environmental externalities from agricultural activities may also have characteristics of non-rivalry (the same good can be consumed by anyone without diminishing the consumption opportunities available to others) and/or non-excludability (the nature of the good is such that it is impossible to exclude anyone from consuming it). When they have these characteristics, they can be defined as agri-environmental public goods. Agri-environmental public goods need not necessarily be desirable; that is, they may cause harm and can be defined as agri-environmental public bads. This book has examined policy measures for agri-environmental public goods in five OECD countries (Australia, Japan, the Netherlands, the United Kingdom and the United States). This is one of the first studies to analyse how each OECD country defines agri-environmental public goods and sets agri-environmental targets and reference levels, and what policies are implemented for targeting which agri-environmental public goods.

Main agri-environmental public goods

Targeted agri-environmental public goods vary depending on the country. This is because various factors such as histories, cultures, climate, farm systems affect the perception of what agri-environmental public goods are. Five agri-environmental public goods (soil protection and quality, water quality, water quantity and availability, air quality and biodiversity) are targeted in the all studied countries. Climate change (greenhouse gas emissions and carbon storage) is a targeted agri-environmental public good except in the United States. Agricultural landscapes are targeted agri-environmental public goods except in Australia. Resilience to natural disasters such as flooding and fire are targeted agri-environmental public goods in Japan, the Netherlands and the United Kingdom, but not in Australia and the United States. Countries' priorities for agri-environmental public goods vary.

These goods, however, do not always have characteristics of non-rivalry and non-excludability. Some environmental externalities from agricultural activities have characteristics of private goods, in which government intervention might not therefore be necessary. It is important to clearly identify environmental externalities from agricultural activities that are important to countries and regions, and examine whether they have the characteristics of non-rivalry and/or non-excludability, and can be defined as agri-environmental public goods (and public bads) in each case.

Farming practices and provision of the agri-environmental public goods

Farm systems, farming practices, farm inputs and agricultural infrastructure (driving forces) affect the provision of agri-environmental public goods (environmental outcomes). It is important to examine how agriculture can provide these agri-environmental public goods, since some farming practices and policy measures bring both positive and negative impacts on the agri-environmental public goods in a different way and degree. It is also important to foster knowledge building and data gathering on the relationship between farming practices and the provision of agri-environmental public goods. This can also facilitate monitoring and the evaluation of policy measures for agri-environmental public goods.

Market failure associated with agri-environmental public goods

Although agriculture can provide agri-environmental public goods, markets for such public goods are, generally speaking, under-developed. This makes it difficult for famers to produce an adequate amount of agri-environmental public goods. Under imperfect markets, the values of agri-environmental public goods are often not reflected in the prices of agricultural commodities and agricultural lands.

Prices are unable to properly convey the value of agri-environmental public goods including their future value, and may result in under/over-supply of agri-environmental public goods.

Nevertheless, the provision of agri-environmental public goods does not necessarily mean governments should always intervene. Although in theory it is difficult to produce an adequate amount of agri-environmental public goods, farmers can provide the right amount incidentally. In addition, government intervention involves additional costs. Benefits from the intervention need to outweigh the costs. To justify the government intervention, evidence of market failure is necessary. However, the cost of not intervening, particularly on the long run, must also be taken into accounts in the cost-benefits analysis.

It is difficult to estimate the scale of demand and supply of agri-environmental public goods because of the absence of markets. As a result, examining whether market failure associated with agri-environmental public goods exists or not is also challenging. The countries studied in this book have all been trying to collect better data on both the demand and supply of agri-environmental public goods. There are some new initiatives that establish networks, include relevant people and institutions, and adopt advanced estimation technics. However, whether the incidental supply of agri-environmental public goods meet demand or not has rarely been examined. This suggests that governments may intervene even in the cases where there are no market failures. There are risks of over-intervention. On the other hand, where market failure exists, there are cases of insufficient or poor government intervention because of lack of information as to the extent of market failure. More efforts are necessary for analysing demand and supply of agri-environmental public goods. This estimation has to be done at an appropriate scale, since some agri-environmental public goods are local public goods while others are regional, national or global public goods.

Cost-benefit analyses generally have not been undertaken because of their technical and political difficulties it can present. Some studies indicate there are cases where the costs of government intervention outweigh its benefits. It is important to avoid government failure. Governments need to take a more rigorous approach to evaluate the benefits and costs of specific policy intervention and of not intervening, and those benefits should be evaluated on the basis of the environmental outcomes, and not according to the use of particular practices. Establishing a coherent monitoring and evaluation framework is also important and it should be done well in advance before government intervention, which gives one to enough time for the monitoring and evaluation. In addition, it is important to examine who gains the most and who loses the most. Benefits and costs are not equally distributed among the parties concerned.

There are some innovative approaches undertaken by private companies, such as payment for ecosystem services in the United Kingdom ("Upstream Thinking Project"). These approaches may be able to overcome market failures and should be better utilised to improve the cost-effectiveness of agri-environmental policies.

Environmental targets and reference levels

Environmental targets and reference levels are useful to discuss who should bear the costs for providing agri-environmental public goods, but they are not clearly defined in many cases. Many financial incentives set reference levels at current farming practices so that governments are required to pay farmers to adopt sustainable farming practices.

In some cases, direct beneficiaries of agri-environmental public goods can be identified. In this case, beneficiaries can bear some of the costs of provision, which can save the costs of government intervention as well as reduce farmers' burden. Community-based approaches or collective action help these people and organisations to be included in the discussion on distribution of burdens.

There must be more discussion on sharing the cost burdens that are associated with providing agri-environmental public goods and avoid paying farmers who cause environmental harms. Before any government intervention, it is necessary to discuss the extent to which farmers should bear the costs and the extent to which taxpayers and consumers should bear the costs. Reference levels and environmental targets should be clearly defined, and environmental targets should be based on generally accepted criteria, such as SMART (Specific, Measurable, Attainable, Realistic and Timely).

Policy measures for the delivery of agri-environmental public goods

Most policy measures target driving forces such as agricultural systems, farming practices, and agricultural infrastructure

Generally speaking, it is easier to target driving forces than environmental outcomes because various factors including non-agricultural ones affect the environmental outcomes. Sometimes, targeting driving forces is the only practical option.

Performance-based policy measures that directly target environmental outcomes are few.

Only two performance-based approaches are reported in the studied countries. The United States Conservation Stewardship Program (CSP) uses a points system to determine a conservation performance for determining payment levels. It establishes scoring tables indicating the relative environmental benefit impact of different practices, but its performance assessment is not based on actual environmental outcomes. The State of Victoria in Australia undertakes pilot projects to enhance habitat conservation on private land by using auctions (conservation tender programmes such as the BushTender programme). As a part of these pilot projects, output based payment for biodiversity conservation has been tried. Farmers are required to meet certain biodiversity conditions for receiving the payments. Learning from these projects can be fruitful for moving to more evidence-based and output-based policy measures. For improving the cost-effectiveness of policy measures, it is important to appropriately target factors that affect the provision of agri-environmental public goods.

Taking into account the heterogeneity of farmers and farmland characteristics and adopting evidence-based approaches can improve the effectiveness of policy measures. Governments should adopt a more evidence-based approach when they develop policy measures for each targeted agri-environmental public good.

The additionality of a policy measure is a key concept to be kept in mind

The additionality of a policy measure is the extent to which the policy is a necessary condition for achieving the environmental target. It is important to avoid paying farmers who would have improved their environmental performance without the payment.

Reducing transaction costs as a result of targeting is a crucial aspect in policy design and choice

Targeting, however, may involve additional transaction costs. They can be reduced by sharing experiences across agencies, regions or countries, exploiting already existing administrative networks, integration of government and private information systems, reducing the number of agencies, and through the use of information technologies.

The fundamental objective of policy measures for agri-environmental public goods is to achieve environmental goals at least overall cost

Policy makers should choose appropriate policy instruments while weighing up the trade-offs between environmental effectiveness, economic efficiency, farmers' compliance costs, administrative costs, transaction costs and other benefits and costs, including consideration of equity and income distribution.

Policy makers should also pay more attention to a wider range of motivations for farmers' actions concerning the environment

Farmers have different perceptions on environmental issues and their preferences and degree of compliance with policy measures differ among them. Traditional policy instruments are sometimes insufficient to overcome the market failure associated with agri-environmental public goods. More research on farmer behaviour and learning from these studies are necessary to develop a holistic approach for agri-environmental public goods. Discussion on best policy mixes and co-ordination among actors is necessary.

Many policy measures target multiple agri-environmental public goods (especially financial incentives such as agri-environmental payments). In addition, each agri-environmental public good is targeted by multiple policy measures. Policy measures for providing agri-environmental public goods are complex sets of various measures because of the history of policy development and the involvement of multiple actors (e.g. ministries, central and local governments, stakeholders). It is not always clear to what extent a particular policy measure tries to address agri-environmental issues, and to what extent other policy measures do so. Reviewing current policy measures and examining whether policy measures create synergies is a first step towards developing better policy mixes.

Annex 6.A Summaries of agri-environmental policy measures in Australia, Japan, the Netherlands, the United Kingdom and the United States

Annex Table 6.A1. Agri-environmental policy measures in Australia

AE public goods	Measures									
	Regulatory			Financial incentives						Facilitative
	Regulatory requirements	Environmental taxes/ Charges	Environmental cross-compliance	Payments based on farming practices	Payments based on land retirement	Payments based on farm fixed assets	Payments based on outcomes	Tradable rights /permits	Community based measures	Technical assistance/ extension/R&D/ labelling/standards/ certification
Water quality	State-based regulations, e.g. for dairy effluent management in Victoria.			CFOC, Reef Rescue, State programs (small temporary payments in all cases)					CFOC	CFOC
Water quantity/ availability								Water markets		
Farmland biodiversity and native vegetation	EBPC Act. State acts for threatened species. State acts limiting clearing of native vegetation.			CFOC, State programs (small temporary payments). Conservation tenders (reverse auctions) programs in Victoria and National Stewardship Program.				BushBroker market for development offsets (Victoria)	CFOC	CFOC
Soil protection/ soil quality	Soil conservation act (state)			CFOC (small temporary payments)					CFOC	CFOC, Community Landcare grants
Climate change– Carbon storage				Carbon Farming initiative						Carbon Farming Futures
Climate change – greenhouse gas emissions				Carbon Farming initiative						
Air quality	Planning restrictions on locations of farms									

CFOC = Caring For Our Country.
Source: Pannell, D. and A. Roberts (2015), “Public Goods and Externalities: Agri-environmental Policy Measures in Australia”.

Annex Table 6.A2. Agri-environmental policy measures in Japan

	Measures									
	Regulatory			Financial incentives						Facilitative
AE public goods	Regulatory requirements	Environmental taxes/ Charges	Environmental cross-compliance	Payments based on farming practices	Payments based on land retirement	Payments based on farm fixed assets	Payments based on outcomes	Tradable rights /permits	Community based measures	Technical assistance/extension/ R&D/ labelling/standards/certification
Agricultural landscapes	Landscape Act			DPFHMA					MCILWE	
Biodiversity	Cartagena Protocol Invasive Alien Species Act		ECC	DPEFF DPFHMA		SDA			MCILWE	SDA LPOA Eco-labelling
Water quality	CWP, AATPULM					SDA AATPULM			MCILWE	SDA LPOA Eco-labelling AATPULM
Water quantity/ availability	River Act			DPFHMA					MCILWE	
Soil quality and protection	ALSPPL					SDA AATPULM			MCILWE	SDA LPOA Eco-labelling SFEA
Climate change – carbon storage			ECC	DPEFF						
Climate change – greenhouse gas emissions								JCS		BIO
Air quality	COO, AATPULM					AATPULM				AATPULM
Resilience to natural disasters				DPFHMA					MCILWE	

Note: Other subsidies are paid for various agri-environmental public goods.

Acronyms: AATPULM – Act on the Appropriate Treatment and Promotion of Utilization of Livestock Manure, ALSPPL – Agricultural Land Soil Pollution Prevention Law , BIO – Biomass Nippon, COO – Control of Offensive Odours, CWP – Control of Water Pollution, DPEFF – Direct Payment for Environmentally Friendly Farming, DPFHMA – Direct Payments to Farmers in Hilly and Mountainous Areas, ECC – Environmental Cross Compliance, JCS- J-Credit Scheme, LPOA – Law on Promotion of Organic Agriculture, SDA – Establishment and Extension of Agricultural Practices that Facilitate the Sustainable Development of Agriculture, SFEA – Soil Fertility Enhancement Act, MCILWE – Measures to Conserve and Improve Land, Water, and the Environment.

Source: Uetake, T. (2015), "Public Goods and Externalities: Agri-environmental Policy Measures in Japan".

Annex Table 6.A3. Agri-environmental policy measures in the Netherlands

AE public goods	Measures									
	Regulatory			Financial incentives						Facilitative
	Regulatory requirements	Environmental taxes/ Charges	Environmental cross-compliance	Payments based on farming practices	Payments based on land retirement	Payments based on farm fixed assets	Payments based on outcomes	Tradable rights /permits	Community based measures	Technical assistance/ extension/ R&D/ labelling/ standards/ certification
Agricultural landscapes	Wro, Boswet	WSH	CC	SNL	SNL			RvG (experimental)	GLB pilots (experimental)	Most facilitative subsidies are on ad hoc basis at present
Biodiversity	FFW, NBW, WBD, HD		CC	SNL, BvN	SNL, BvN	MIA + Vamil		RGP	GLB pilots (experimental)	B+B, CI, TSAF
Water quality	MW, WW, WBB. ND, IPPCD, WFD		CC							
Water quantity/ availability	WW, WSW, WFD	WSH	CC	GBDA	GBDA					
Soil protection and quality	WW		CC							
Climate change – carbon storage						MIA + Vamil			TSAF	TSAF
Climate change – greenhouse gas emissions	NECD	MH	CC			MIA + Vamil		RED	TSAF	TSAF, TST
Air quality	WAV /WM, NECD		CC			MIA + Vamil				SP
Resilience to flooding			CC							FD

Acronyms: B+B –Biodiversiteit en Bedrijfsleven (Biodiversity and Business), Boswet (Forest Act), BvN – Boeren voor Natuur (Farming for Nature), CC – Cross Compliance, CI – Cooperation and Innovation , FD – (EC) Flood Directive, FFW – Flora en Faunawet (Flora and Fauna Act) , GBDA – GroenBlauwe dooradering (Green veins), GLB pilots – pilots gemeenschappelijk landbouwbeleid (Common Agricultural Policy pilots), HD – (EC) Habitats Directive, IPPCD – (EC) Integrated Pollution Prevention and Control Directive, NBW – Natuurbeschermingswet (Nature Protection Act), ND – (EC) Nitrates Directive, NECD – (EC) National Emission Ceiling Directive, MIA + Vamil – Milieu Investeringsaftrek + willekeurige afschrijving milieuinvesteringen (Environmental tax reduction programmes), MH – Milieuheffing (Environmental levy on energy / fuel) MW – Meststoffenwet (Fertilizer application law), RED – (EC) Renewable Energy Directive, RGP – Regeling GroenProjecten (Green Projects – fiscal arrangement for green projects), RvG – Rood voor Groen (Red for Green), SNL – Subsidieregeling Natuur en Landschap (Subsidies scheme for Nature and Landscape), SP – Subsidieregeling Praktijknetwerken (Subsidy for Community of Practise to reduce ammonia emissions), TSAF – TopSector AgroFood, TST – Topsector Tuinbouw (Topsector Horticulture), WAV – Wet Ammoniak en veehouderij (Ammonia and Livestock Act) , WBB – Wet bodembescherming (Soil Protection Act) , WBD – (EC) Wild Birds Directive, WFD – (EC) Water Framework Directive, WM – Wet milieubeheer (Environmental Management act), Wro – Wet ruimtelijke ordening (Spatial planning act), WSH – Waterschapsheffing (Water board districts levy), WSW – Waterschapswet (Water Board District Act), WW – Waterwet (Water act).

Source: Schrijver, R. and T. Uetake (2015), "Public Goods and Externalities: Agri-environmental Policy Measures in the Netherlands".

Annex Table 6.A4. Agri-environmental policy measures in the United Kingdom

AE public goods	Measures									
	Regulatory			Financial incentives						Facilitative
	Regulatory requirements	Environmental taxes/ charges	Environmental cross-compliance	Payments based on farming practices	Payments based on land retirement	Payments based on farm fixed assets	Payments based on outcomes	Tradable rights /permits	Community based measures	Technical assistance/extension /R&D/ labelling/standards/certification
Agricultural landscapes			CC	ES, Glastir, RDC, NICMS	EWGS, Glastir, RDC, WGS	RDC				FAS, FATI/ETIP, FC, WFR, CAFRE
Biodiversity	WCA, CROW, WBD, HD		CC	ES, Glastir, RDC, NICMS	EWGS, Glastir, RDC, WGS					FAS, FATI/ETIP, FC, WFR, CAFRE
Water quality/ availability	WRA, ND, IPPCD, WFD		CC	ES, Glastir, RDC, NICMS	EWGS, Glastir, RDC, WGS	ECSFDI, Glastir, RDC, FMP				FAS, FATI/ETIP, FC WFR, CAFRE
Water quantity	WRA		CC			FFIS		Water rights trading		FAS, FC, WFR, CAFRE
Soil quality and protection			CC	ES, Glastir, NICMS		FFIS				FAS, FATI/ETIP, FC, WFR, CAFRE
Climate change – carbon storage				ES, Glastir, RDC, NICMS	EWGS, Glastir, RDC, WGS					FAS, FC, WFR
Climate change – greenhouse gas emissions	NECD			ES, RDC, NICMS		FFIS, Glastir, RDC, FMP				FAS, FC, WFR
Air quality	EPA, CAA, NECD			NICMS						
Resilience to natural disasters – flooding				ES, Glastir	EWGS, Glastir, RDC, WGS					FC
Fire			CC							

Notes: Acts/programmes listed in the following order: England, Wales, Scotland and Northern Ireland.

Acronyms: CAA – Clean Air Act, CAFRE – College of Agriculture Food and Rural Enterprise, CC – Cross Compliance, CROW – Countryside and Rights of Way Act, ECSFDI – England Catchment Sensitive Farming Delivery Initiative, ES – Environmental Stewardship, EWGS – England Woodland Grant Scheme, FAS – Farming Advice Service, FATI/ETIP – Farm Advice Training and Information / ELS (Entry Level Stewardship) Training and Information Programme, FC – Farming Connect, FFIS – Farming and Forestry Improvement Scheme, FMP – Farm Modernisation Programme, HD – (EC) Habitats Directive, IPPCD – (EC) Integrated Pollution Prevention and Control Directive, ND – (EC) Nitrates Directive, NECD – (EC) National Emission Ceiling Directive, NICMS – Northern Ireland Countryside Management Scheme, RDC – Rural Development Contracts, WBD – (EC) Wild Birds Directive, WCA – Wildlife and Countryside Act, WFD – (EC) Water Framework Directive, WFR – Whole Farm Review, WGS – Woodland Grant Scheme, WRA – Water Resources Act.

Source: Jones, J., P. Silcock and T. Uetake (2015), "Public Goods and Externalities: Agri-environmental Policy Measures in the United Kingdom".

Annex Table 6.A5. Agri-environmental policy measures in the United States

AE public goods	Measures									
	Regulatory			Financial incentives						Facilitative
	Regulatory requirements	Environ-mental taxes/ Charges	Environmental cross-compliance	Payments based on farming practices	Payments based on land retirement	Payments based on farm fixed assets	Payments based on outcomes/ performance rankings	Tradable rights /permits	Com-munity based measures	Technical assistance/ extension/ R&D/ labelling/ standards/ certification
Soil quality			USDA Highly Erodible Land and Wetlands Conservation (Sodbuster)	USDA EQIP Some states	USDA Land Retirement Programs (CRP)		USDA Conservation Stewardship Program (CSP)			Various federal, state and local educational programs, federal and state technical assistance programs, federal organic labelling requirements
Water quality	Pesticides (federal); Regulated concentrated animal feeding operations (federal and state); Farming practices (e.g. nutrient management) (some states)	Agricultural privilege tax (Florida)		USDA EQIP Some states	USDA Land Retirement Programs (CRP)		USDA (CSP)	Water quality trading (some states)		
Water quantity	Laws and regulations governing access to water, and water use vary across and within states	Water pricing		USDA EQIP	USDA Land Retirement Programs (CREP) in some states		USDA (CSP)	Water Markets		
Wetlands	Federal and state laws governing wetland draining and filling		USDA Highly Erodible Lands and Wetlands (Swampbuster)		USDA Land Retirement Programs (CRP/CREP/ACEP)		USDA (CSP)	Wetlands Mitigation Banking		
Wildlife	Federal and state laws protection for endangered species habitat		-USDA Crop Production on Native Sod (sodsaver) Some states	USDA EQIP	USDA Land Retirement Programs (CRP/ CREP)		USDA (CSP)	Conserva -tion Mitigation Banking		
Air quality	Emissions of criteria pollutants (California)			USDA EQIP	USDA Land Retirement Programs (CRP)		USDA (CSP)			
Agricultural landscapes preservation	State and local land use zoning		-USDA Crop Production on Native Sod (sodsaver) Some states	USDA conservation easements (ACEP); State and local preservation programs						

Acronyms: ACEP – Agricultural Conservation Easement Program CREP – Conservation Reserve Enhancement Program, CRP – Conservation Reserve Program, CSP – Conservation Stewardship Program, EQIP – Environmental Quality Incentives Program.

Source: Adapted from Shortle, J. and T. Uetake (2015), "Public Goods and Externalities: Agri-environmental Policy Measures in the United States".

ORGANISATION FOR ECONOMIC CO-OPERATION AND DEVELOPMENT

The OECD is a unique forum where governments work together to address the economic, social and environmental challenges of globalisation. The OECD is also at the forefront of efforts to understand and to help governments respond to new developments and concerns, such as corporate governance, the information economy and the challenges of an ageing population. The Organisation provides a setting where governments can compare policy experiences, seek answers to common problems, identify good practice and work to co-ordinate domestic and international policies.

The OECD member countries are: Australia, Austria, Belgium, Canada, Chile, the Czech Republic, Denmark, Estonia, Finland, France, Germany, Greece, Hungary, Iceland, Ireland, Israel, Italy, Japan, Korea, Luxembourg, Mexico, the Netherlands, New Zealand, Norway, Poland, Portugal, the Slovak Republic, Slovenia, Spain, Sweden, Switzerland, Turkey, the United Kingdom and the United States. The European Union takes part in the work of the OECD.

OECD Publishing disseminates widely the results of the Organisation's statistics gathering and research on economic, social and environmental issues, as well as the conventions, guidelines and standards agreed by its members.

OECD PUBLISHING, 2, rue André-Pascal, 75775 PARIS CEDEX 16
(51 2015 17 1 P) ISBN 978-92-64-23979-1 – 2015-17

www.ingramcontent.com/pod-product-compliance
Lightning Source LLC
LaVergne TN
LVHW081417110826
845149LV00010B/1768

* 9 7 8 9 2 6 4 2 3 9 7 9 1 *